Under the Shadow

To order additional copies of

UNDER THE SHADOW,

by

Mary Hui-Tze Wong,

call

1-800-765-6955.

Visit us at

www.reviewandherald.com

for information on other Review and Herald® products.

Under the SHADOW

MARY HUI-TZE WONG
WITH **MAYLAN SCHURCH**

REVIEW AND HERALD® PUBLISHING ASSOCIATION
HAGERSTOWN, MD 21740

The Review and Herald® Publishing Association publishes biblically based materials for spiritual, physical, and mental growth and Christian discipleship.

The author assumes full responsibility for the accuracy of all facts and quotations as cited in this book.

Unless otherwise noted, Bible texts in this book are from the *Holy Bible, New International Version*. Copyright © 1973, 1978, 1984, International Bible Society. Used by permission of Zondervan Bible Publishers.

This book was
Edited by Gerald Wheeler
Cover design and illustration by Trent Truman
Interior designed by Candy Harvey
Electronic makeup by Shirley M. Bolivar
Typeset: 11/14 Bembo

PRINTED IN U.S.A.

11 10 09 08 07   5 4 3 2 1

R&H Cataloging Service
Under the shadow
    A story of narrow escapes and God's protecting hand.
By Mary Hui-Tze and Maylan Schurch.

    1. Chong Joshua Yun Foh, 1911-1999.   I. Schurch, Maylan, 1950-   .
II. Title.

951

ISBN 0-8280-1938-X
ISBN 978-0-8280-1938-5

Dedication

To my parents,

Joshua Yun Foh Chong and Eunice Tshin Chin Chong,
whose life of dedication to God made possible the contents of this book.

Contents

1 Child Bride / 11

2 Surviving the Black Death / 18

3 Yun Foh's Birth and Early Childhood / 24

4 Rendezvous at Au Mi San / 28

5 Student Radical / 34

6 From Death's Shadow to Greater Light / 40

7 In Training for the Master's Service / 46

8 Missionary to the Land of the Headhunters / 51

9 Sarawak / 58

10 Invaded by Air and Sea / 64

11 Enemy Occupation / 70

12 When Death Rained Out of the Sky / 76

13 Liberation! / 81

14 A Step Ahead of the Red Tide / 87

15 In Active Service / 99

16 Joy and Sacrifice in Singapore / 106

17 Escape From Vietnam / 115

18 Sunset and Eventide / 122

Acknowledgments

F OR THE SUCCESSFUL COMPLETION of this book I wish to give honor and praise to God for the miracles featured in this book and to express my gratitude and deep appreciation to the following individuals:

My coauthor, Pastor Maylan Schurch, for applying his expertise and suggestions to highlight this story's drama.

The acquisition editor of the Review and Herald Publishing Association, Jeannette Johnson, for her encouragement and suggestions.

My aunt, Mrs. Sue Ting, for reading to me the voluminous notes left by Dad and filling me in on the details regarding the early years of his and Grandmother's lives.

My husband, David Wong, for his encouragement and for helping to prepare the photographs included in the book.

My cousin, Michael Chang, for supplying me with the details of his narrow escape from Vietnam.

"He that dwelleth in the secret place
of the most High shall abide
under the shadow of the Almighty."
—*Psalm 91:1, KJV*

1

Child Bride

The year is 1898.

C. S. Lewis is born this year, and Alice in Wonderland *author Lewis Carroll dies. H. G. Wells first publishes* The War of the Worlds, *which when rewritten as a radio drama four decades later will frighten much of America. A Japanese bacteriologist named Shiga identifies the dysentery bacillus, and Pierre and Marie Curie discover radium.*

Sprawling across Asia like a wide, happy smile, the mysterious country of China feels at its borders the meddling of England and Russia. At the edge of the smile's lower lip is the city of Guangzhou, just north of Hong Kong. And 300 miles from Guangzhou, in a tiny village, a 7-year-old girl whose Chinese name means "plum blossom" is blissfully unaware that her life is about to change forever.

"MEI HWA, COME QUICKLY," Mother called. "Papa is ready."

Eyes sparkling, the child hurried to her mother's side. The only daughter in a wealthy family that included two sons, she was thrilled that her father was taking her—and not her brothers—on a trip to the next village.

Without a word Mother handed her a small bag. As Mei Hwa looked inside, her mouth dropped open. The bag contained two suits of new clothes, a pair of new sandals, and some jewelry—earrings, a ring, a necklace, an anklet, and a bracelet.

"All these for me?" The girl looked up into her mother's eyes and was startled to see tears flooding them. "Mama, why are you crying?"

"Yes, all these are for you," Mother said, answering the first question and ignoring the second. An incredible sadness filled her voice.

But Mei Hwa was too excited to give it much thought. From bits of conversation she'd overheard, she knew they'd be visiting a family named Chong. She'd never met them and had no idea why the trip would make Mother cry. So she didn't worry, but continued to think excitedly about the journey ahead.

This will be the first time I've set foot outside our village, she thought to herself. *And my two noisy brothers won't be along. It will be just Papa and me. And when I am tired, he'll carry me on his strong back, because I'm only 7.*

Beaming with excitement—and totally oblivious to the sorrow ahead—Mei Hwa waved goodbye to her mother and brothers and set out eagerly beside Papa. Even though by then trains and bicycles had come to China, most people still traveled from one village to another on foot, and during the next few days more than 50 miles passed under Papa's and Mei Hwa's sandals.

Finally the travel-worn figures arrived at their destination.

Though she was tired, the girl still gazed with delight at the Chong family home, a red brick building that nestled at the foot of a hill. At the back of the house the river meandered lazily over a landscape dotted with weeping willow, cherry, and plum trees. The grain fields had by now turned golden. The girl's eyes followed the slope of the hill to the seven-story pagoda fringed by green bamboo fronds that perched on its summit. The building gave the village below its name, Tap Kong Ha (pagoda village).

"Papa," Mei Hwa whispered, tugging on his hand.

"What?"

Eyes wide, she stared around her. "The Chongs must be very rich."

Her father swallowed and nodded. "They are well-to-do."

And indeed they were. Now that she was closer, the girl could see that the red brick building was actually one of several houses, all built around a huge courtyard.

Someone noticed their arrival, and quickly a crowd of people gathered to greet them. Soon Mei Hwa found herself in the courtyard. In the center of it was a small pond filled with fish and pink and white water lilies. Bonsai and other miniature plants ringed the pond.

Chatting shyly with the children, she discovered that each of the smaller dwellings housed a Chong son and his family. One building was a huge kitchen in which the daughters-in-law of the family cooked, chatted, and quarreled noisily. Squawking children chased each other between the piles of firewood stacked haphazardly near the stove and the baskets of vegetables and grain scattered on the floor.

For two days an air of festivity pervaded the Chong home. But early on the third morning Papa gently shook Mei Hwa awake and held her briefly in his arms. In his eyes she noticed a deep sadness that reminded her of what she had seen in her mother's face.

"Mei—" he began, then stopped and softly cleared his throat. "Mei Hwa, my . . . my dear child. It is—time for me to leave now. You—you remember to take good care of yourself." His voice trailed away.

"Wait a minute, Papa. I have not packed my things yet." She jumped out of bed.

"No, Mei Hwa." His voice shook. Again he cleared his throat, and suddenly he forced his words out, quickly and desperately. "You—you will not be going home with me. You are—here to stay. You have now become the new bride in the Chong family, and this will be your new home."

"What?" The girl couldn't believe her ears. "I'm not going back to Mother?"

"No," he said, shaking his head. "You are a bride."

Cradled in his arms, she stared at him, bewildered. "A *bride?*"

He nodded, then began to tremble. Quickly he set her down on the floor. Instantly she scrambled to her feet and clutched his legs. "Papa, don't go!"

With trembling hands he tried to remove her grasping fingers.

"Papa, what is a bride?" Mei Hwa had no idea of what the word meant except for images of girls dressed in their red flowing robes and crowned with huge red headgear, their eyes peering from behind thick veils on their wedding day.

The images vanished abruptly as she felt her father pulling away.

Papa is leaving me in this totally unfamiliar place? How could he?

It was too much for her to grasp. Terrified, she clung to him, but he gently shook her free. Tears streaming down his face, he looked down at her, then walked away without a backward glance.

For the rest of the day Mei Hwa wept uncontrollably. She felt abandoned—betrayed.

She didn't know that all this time someone had been furtively watching her from the shadows. Eleven-year-old Sook Au, the Chong family's fourth son, couldn't understand the distress of the pretty little girl. His family had told him that she was his new bride, and even though he didn't fully understand what that meant, he was eager to get acquainted with her.

"It'll be fun to have her as a new playmate," he told himself. "If only she didn't cry so much!"

That night Mei Hwa fell into a troubled sleep, only to be awakened again early the next morning by someone shaking her shoulders. It was Mrs. Chong, her new mother-in-law.

"Get up, girl!" the woman ordered. "Go fetch me water to wash my face and feet!"

Staggering upright, Mei Hwa groped her way out through the darkness to the well. Grasping a small bucket with a narrow rope tied to it, she let it fall into the water, and almost tumbled sleepily in after it. Then pulling the bucket up again, she stumbled back into the house, found a small basin, and filled it with water mingled with her tears. She then took it to mother-in-law's bedchamber. Clumsily she splashed some water onto the woman's feet.

"You stupid girl!" Mrs. Chong shrieked. "The water is freezing cold! You should have brought me hot water."

The next morning Mei Hwa took special pains to fill the basin with hot water, but the minute her mother-in-law's feet touched the scalding liquid she kicked the basin away with an angry scream.

Thus began Mei Hwa's life as a child bride in the home of her betrothed. Every morning started with the ritual of washing her mother-in-law's feet, followed by a day of backbreaking work in the grain fields or around the house.

In her parents' home she'd been pampered and well fed, but now her stomach always growled with hunger pangs. Even though she and her sisters-in-law prepared many large dishes of chicken, roast pork, and vegetables in the kitchen, they had to watch in envy as the men enjoyed the food during mealtimes in the common dining room. Whatever remained then went to the kitchen for the women and the children—the older ones eating first.

It meant that there was little left for Mei Hwa and her sisters-in-law. At times when hunger kept her from sleeping, the girl would creep out of her bed in the darkness and slip into the shack where the family kept the piles of harvested yams, and she would chew on them until the pangs subsided. Homesickness also gnawed at her, but her only hope of seeing her family was once a year when her in-laws would allow her to visit on Chinese New Year's Day.

Nine years crawled by. Then it came time for her and Sook Au to consummate their marriage. After a formal wedding feast during which she wore the red wedding gown and headgear, she moved in with her husband in the annex assigned him.

Before a year was over, Mei Hwa felt sick to her stomach.

"What's wrong?" one of her older sisters-in-law asked her at mealtime.

Mei Hwa shrugged. "I don't know. As soon as I set eyes on food, I lose my appetite."

The sister-in-law raised her eyebrows. "You're pregnant," she stated bluntly.

And sure enough, Mei Hwa was indeed carrying a new life inside her. Each day the baby grew bigger, and soon she could feel it kicking.

"This first child had better be a boy," a sister-in-law warned. "If you have a girl, life's going to be miserable for both you and the child."

Mei Hwa swallowed.

"Girls are bad investments," the older girl continued. "Our families have to spend money and time in raising us, only to see us married off to other families to bear children for them. Boys are *good* investments."

Worriedly Mei Hwa's hand moved to the bulge in her tummy.

"Boys stay in the ancestral home," the sister-in-law went on, "and they marry daughters-in-law who will help with the housework. And the daughters-in-law will have children who will carry on the family name. And if the family has enough money, it's the boys who go to school and get an education."

Surely the gods can help me here, Mei Hwa thought as she desperately wended her way to the nearest temple. "Please!" she groaned as she prostrated herself and waved the joss sticks before the fierce-looking gods with their bushy eyebrows and spadelike mustaches curling around their thick red lips. "Please! Please let it be a boy. I promise I will bring you lots of offerings."

Through the months that followed she awaited the birth of the baby with great anxiety. Eight months had dragged by, and then nine, but without any sign of the baby coming.

Her sisters-in-law ran their hands over her abdomen. "Yes! It's a boy!" they exclaimed gleefully.

"How can you tell?" Mei Hwa asked anxiously.

"By the shape."

"Well, I hope he's born soon," she moaned. "It's exhausting carrying him around in the grain fields."

One night as the tenth month drew to an end, Mei Hwa felt streaks of agony surge through her body, threatening to tear her apart. The family hurriedly summoned the village midwife. Moaning loudly, Mei Hwa writhed and pushed through the long hours of the night, but the baby refused to budge. All this time the midwife hunched over her, loudly calling out, "Push! Push! Harder! Harder!" Just when Mei Hwa thought she would die of exhaustion and pain, the lusty cry of a 10-pound red-faced baby pierced the air. Mother Chong chortled with delight as the midwife gently put the baby into her arms. It was a boy!

For a full month after that Mei Hwa relished the special treatment accorded her after a male's birth. The family would not permit her to do any work except to nurse her baby and to keep herself warm in the bedroom. Her sisters-in-law fed her a thin soup made of chicken steamed with ginger, wine, or Chinese herbs so that she would recover her strength to bear more babies. When the baby was a month old, the Chong clan had a huge feast to celebrate the event, and presented hard-boiled eggs dyed red to relatives, friends, and neighbors.

Before her son, Yun Mook, was able to walk, Mei Hwa was again big with child. Surely her prayers to the idols had been answered, because the next baby was also a boy! Once more she received special treatment, and her status in the Chong household rose. Those who had not borne a male child looked on her with envy and respect. Remembering her promise to the gods, she frequently visited the temple to take them offerings of food, rice, and money. Then two more babies followed, this time girls, but it didn't matter, since she already had two sons.

"Ah! Life is good." Sook Au sighed with contentment one day.

As he watched his little brood of four children playing around him, he reflected on the blessings that he was enjoying. Though unable to read and write—because girls weren't educated in those days—his wife, Mei Hwa, had been most fruitful.

"I'm lucky," he said to himself, "not to have a wife like Mei Ling." Married for 10 years to his brother Sook Wen, the sister-in-law was still childless. In those days people considered infertility the woman's fault, and Mother Chong had constantly hounded her daughter-in-law to bear a child.

Mei Ling had done her part. She'd made the rounds of the temples to pray to the gods, but they seemed to have turned a deaf ear. So Mother Chong began to pressure Sook Wen to marry a second wife so that his line of the family would continue.

"But *I* am lucky," Sook Au said to himself. "I don't have a thing to worry about. I've graduated from high school with distinction. And now all I have to do is to study hard and prepare to take the national examination. And when I pass it, I'll be an administrator in the government." He shuddered slightly. "No, the life of a farmer isn't for me. I'm going to join the ranks of the elite and make a name for myself."

To ensure his success in the examinations, he decided to journey to where he could find manuscripts to study and tutoring to prepare him for the tests. Mei Hwa had to go along with him to make sure that he was fed and had enough rest. Even though she sighed at the prospect of leaving her husband's now-familiar ancestral home, she packed up and, together with him and their four youngsters, left for the distant town.

After a year of preparations Sook Au and his family returned to Tap Kong Ha. He was all set to enjoy the bright days ahead of him. However, he had no way of seeing the dark clouds looming on the horizon.

2

Surviving the Black Death

"AIYA! AIYO!"

Sook Au lurched upward out of a deep sleep.

"I'm going to kill that rooster," he muttered, "and have him for lunch."

"Aiya! Aiyo! Yen wong ah!" (Alas! Help!)

The cry that stabbed the air hadn't been a rooster after all. With a sick feeling in his stomach Sook Au listened to the loud, mournful wailing. It sounded as though it was coming from the house next door, and it meant that someone in his neighbor's house was dying.

Each day now for the past month he had heard similar wails from different parts of the village, followed by mournful funeral processions. *Now it's near,* he thought. *Too near. Too close to my family.* More frightening still, in some cases several funeral processions had emerged from the same house. With a family's first death the funeral was elaborate, with the clashing cymbals and haunting flutes of a band, and a long procession of mourners—spouse, children, grandchildren in their white burlap mourning garb and black armbands, accompanied by a retinue of friends and well-wishers—marching through the village.

However, with each subsequent death in the same family the wailing become weaker, the funeral less elaborate, and the mourners fewer, with hardly anyone outside of the family circle present. No funeral followed the final death. Someone either quietly pulled the corpse outside the door in the dark of night to be taken away for burial, or the body would simply be left in the house to decompose.

Sook Au shook the last shreds of sleep away and stumbled to his feet. As he stared out at the village pond that morning, fear reached its chilling fingers deep into him. The water in the pond was blood red—another bad omen that something terrible had overtaken his home village. The mysterious illness began with a burning fever and ended with an excruciatingly painful death. Whole families perished within a short time. The village was in the grip of the plague—the Black Death.

"Mei Hwa," he called. "I've made a decision."

His wife hurried to his side. Her eyes reflected the fear in his.

"We must flee," he told her.

"But where?"

"To your parents' home. It's 50 miles away. Maybe that's far enough to be safe."

While Mei Hwa threw some of their clothes and belongings into backpacks, Sook Au hurried to the dwellings of his parents and brothers. "Come with us," he urged.

But they refused. "Don't worry," they said. "Your brother Sook Wen is the village doctor. He'll know what to do if anyone in the family gets sick." However, as Sook Au led his family away from the village, he had a premonition that it would be the last time he would see his relatives alive.

"Hurry!" he urged his little ones as they struggled to keep up with his long strides. It would be a journey of several days, and the children were not used to traveling great distances on foot. From time to time he or his wife would have to carry them on their backs, and though their shoulders drooped with exhaustion and worry, Sook Au felt death breathing down his neck and wanted to put as much distance as he could between himself and his home village.

Intermittent news reached him from his home village during the next few weeks—and then came the chilling word that his older brother, the village physician, had contracted the plague while attending the sick. The doctor was unable to heal himself, and soon they had to bury him.

It took months before Sook Au was able to learn the details of what had actually happened to the rest of his family.

"It's time now to get out of the village," Father Chong had solemnly announced to his family after they had buried Sook Wen. Their hearts breaking from their new loss, the grieving family began the journey along the dirt road to the neighboring village. As with Sook Au and Mei Hwa, the urgency of putting distance between themselves and their home village drove them on, but suddenly they discovered that Sook Hong, the second brother, had begun to lag behind.

"Wait! Not so fast!" he kept repeating. His eyes had turned bloodshot, and his breath came in ragged puffs. As soon as the family had checked into an inn halfway to the next town, he threw himself on the bed. Soon he burned with fever and tossed in delirium.

Early the next morning Father Chong announced, "It is no use for us to go on." His voice filled with despair, he said, "Our fate has been sealed. We must turn back home to await death. The gods must have been unhappy with our offerings, because their wrath and curse are upon us and our village."

Recognizing the futility of going on and resigned to the fate that awaited them, the family agreed, and retraced their steps home. Death claimed Sook Hong soon after their return. The third brother, Sook Tin, was next. Their wives and children also succumbed, and then finally Father and Mother Chong. All were gone in a matter of weeks.

And no one had been able to pass on the news to Sook Au. Anxiety gnawed at him as he awaited word from home. Deep in his heart he knew the reason for the silence: his family had perished from the plague! One day as tears coursed down his cheeks, Mei Hwa tried to comfort him, and he embraced her.

"I should be back at our village," he said through clenched teeth. "According to custom, I should pay my respects to the dead. I should burn incense and paper money. I should buy the little paper houses and furniture items and burn them at the graves of my mother and father and brothers so they'll be well provided for in the netherworld."

His wife waited in silence.

"But what would you and the family do," he continued, "if I caught the disease too and joined my parents in death?" He shook his head, and his embrace tightened. "No," he said firmly. "We have four children, and one is still a babe in arms. I will not desert you. *You* need me, not they."

So they stayed in his in-laws' village until he received notice that the epidemic had ceased. "There is no further evidence of the plague in the village," the message said, "and your house has been fumigated. You may return."

20

Ten months to the day after he had left his home village, Sook Au and his little family stood on the threshold of his family house. A wave of silence greeted him. All he saw was the dusty array of family gods and goddesses—Ch'eng-Huang, god of moats and walls; Men-shen, gods of the double doorway; Kwan Yin, goddess of mercy and compassion; T'shai-shen, god of wealth; and Fu-shen Tsao, god of happiness.

Sook Au glared at the gods with rising rage. *Where were you,* he silently asked them, *when all my family was sick?*

They gazed back at him with their blind eyes.

Where were you? he repeated. *Didn't we faithfully set rich offerings of rice, meat, flowers, and other delicacies at each of your altars? Didn't we carefully put up shrines for you in different parts of the house? Didn't we worship at your village shrines? Was our devotion to you in vain?*

Suddenly Sook Au strode up to the gods. While his wife and children watched wide-eyed from the doorway, he snatched the images unceremoniously from their pedestals and tossed them one by one into the trash can. "My mind is made up," he said aloud. "From now on I'm going to find and serve a god who can *truly* take care of my family and me."

In a daze Mei Hwa began preparing a simple meal for the family. *What on earth is my husband doing?* she asked herself, glancing wonderingly at him from time to time. *These are the same gods who answered my petitions when as a young bride I prayed for sons!*

"You are searching for another god?" she asked casually.

"I am."

"And where will you find him?"

"I have an idea," he replied. "Remember that group of people who were meeting in a building in your parents' village?"

"The people who sang?"

He nodded. "The Christians. The ones who call themselves Lutherans. Do you remember how soothing their music sounded? And every time their pastor came to visit your parents, I listened while he talked about his God. He said that his God was greater than all the gods that we have worshipped."

"But how do you know this is true?"

"I don't *know* it is true," he admitted, "but now that our own gods have proved worthless to protect us from pestilence and death, I have the right to try this new god."

21

The very next Sunday Sook Au visited the church in his home village. The pastor persuaded him to take regular Bible studies, and he and his family were soon baptized.

"Through this family tragedy," Sook Au would tell others in later years, "God not only gave us the consolation and hope we needed, but led us out of the darkness of idolatry into the light of truth. I decided that from then on, there was no turning back."

In the days following their return to the village, Sook Au took his mind off his grief by throwing himself into the final preparations for the national examination that the plague had so tragically and suddenly interrupted.

But God had other plans for his life.

"Papa," Yun Mook, the oldest boy, said one day, "here's a letter for you."

A letter? Sook Au thought. *That's strange.* Since he seldom received any letters, he tore open the envelope eagerly.

"Mr. Chong," the letter began, "we have the pleasure of offering to you a full scholarship to join the Lutheran Teacher's Institute in Guangzhou. Upon your graduation from the institute, we hope that you will teach in one of the mission schools run by the Lutheran Church. If you are interested in accepting the scholarship, please fill in the enclosed application forms and return them to us as soon as you can." The letter was signed with the name of Lu Wah Dek, education director.

As though hypnotized, Sook Au stood staring at the letter. His mind raced over what he knew about the Lutherans. Headquartered in Guangzhou at that time, the denomination had established numerous mission schools, as well as schools for those who were blind, in many parts of China and Hong Kong. Evidently Sook Au's pastor, sensing his abilities, had passed his name on to church leadership.

The letter fluttered to the floor.

What? he thought to himself. *Give up my dreams of an elite government post to become a lowly teacher?*

"Unthinkable," he said aloud.

Though Mei Hwa looked at him curiously, he said nothing more, but picked up the letter, folded it, and put it away.

But in the days that followed, a struggle raged inside him. *I'm preparing to take the national exam,* he fumed to himself. *I'm going to become a government officer, a mandarin. I'm going to be rich, and I'm going to enjoy prestige and honor. And I'm finally going to be able to provide for my family.*

On the other hand, he had a strong feeling that the Christian God must have some special plan for him, because out of all his family members, God had saved him from the plague. And the institute was not far away, so his family wouldn't have to move from the ancestral home while he studied.

More than that, he mused, *Christ Himself gave up His own life in order to offer me the hope of eternity. And in many of our Lutheran churches and schools are foreign missionaries who've been willing to leave their homelands and loved ones to come to China to teach and to preach the gospel. Now that my God and my church need my service, how can I turn my back on them?*

"God," he cried out in great perplexity, "is this what You want me to do? You know that I need money to provide well for my family. If I become a mere teacher, my income will not be enough to support their needs. What will I do then?"

But a passage from the Christian Scriptures echoed in his mind: "Seek first his kingdom and his righteousness, and all these things will be given to you as well" (Matt. 6:33). Wasn't this a promise that if he took care of God's business, God would provide all his needs?

But if I take this road, will I be honoring the memory of my deceased parents? he asked himself. *They had placed a great deal of hope in my passing the national exam and making a name for myself.*

Finally, after a great deal of prayer and deliberation, Sook Au made his decision. He would enroll in the two-year program at the teacher's training institute and dedicate his life, not to the government, but to God.

Upon his graduation from the institute, the Lutheran mission leadership sent him to Singlin, a small town nearby, to teach in an elementary school. But before he saw the fulfillment of the promise that God would provide for him and his family, his faith would face a severe test.

3

Yun Foh's Birth and Early Childhood

HER ARMS WEAK from hunger, Mei Hwa scraped the bottom of the rice barrel for the last few grains. Putting as much water as she could into the pot, she boiled the tiny quantity of rice into a thin porridge that she would serve to her family with salted duck's egg or preserved vegetables.

My stomach is growling, she thought, *but I have to feed my husband and children first. Then I'll take what's left—which is often nothing.*

Her constant hunger reminded her of her early days as a child bride. Didn't Sook Au notice that she did her best to feed the rest of the family before thinking of her own needs? Couldn't he see that she was always hungry?

It's even harder to bear the hunger pangs now that I'm pregnant again. The baby seems to be forever kicking—it's telling me that it is hungry too. In a few more months we'll have an additional mouth to feed.

Directing a worried look at her husband, she ventured, "Sook Au, the last of our rice is gone."

He glanced at her. "Well, buy some more."

"I have no more money."

"What? All the money *gone?*" he exploded. "You need to be more careful with what I have given you!"

Bowing her head, she said quietly, "I have an idea."

"What idea?"

"There's a plot of land on the school compound," she said hesitantly. "Maybe I could get permission from the principal to start a vegetable garden."

She heard him hiccup with astonishment, but quickly hurried on. "That way I could supplement our diet with the vegetables I grow, and with the money I save, I can buy more rice."

"What are you thinking of?" he demanded. "It will be a loss of face for me if my colleagues and students see my wife working in a vegetable garden! *No.*"

Then seeing the color drain from her face and the tears threatening to overflow, he regretted his hasty words. "Well . . . uh . . . I suppose . . . you could give it a try."

By the time he had said the final syllables, he found himself alone. Mei Hwa had shot out of the door and headed for the principal's office. With not only her husband's but the principal's permission in hand, she got the seedlings she needed. Day after day she and the children worked diligently in the little vegetable garden. She also began to raise some chickens to provide eggs for her children. And soon the family didn't feel their stomachs growl as they had before.

Once he'd become used to the idea of a gardening wife, Sook Au did his part in trying to help the family conserve what little resources they had. He reminded them of the importance of thrift and seized every opportunity to tell them stories that emphasized the value of financial prudence.

"Remember the story of Jesus feeding the 5,000?" he asked. "Remember how all the leftover food was not wasted but collected?" He also pointed them to the examples of other teachers and church leaders who modeled thrift and self-sacrifice.

On April 17, 1911, a new baby boy joined the family. They named him Yun Foh (eternal peace). As Mei Hwa gazed down at the third boy in her family she worried, *Where will I get food for this scrawny baby? It's hard enough to feed our four older children.*

Colleagues and friends hurried over to see the little newborn. "What a tiny baby he is," they commented. "He will need a lot of milk to grow stronger and fatter." With a smile Mei Hwa nodded. *But where's the milk going to come from?* she asked herself.

Almost immediately someone else knocked at the door. It was the missionary's wife. "Oh, this baby is too tiny," she exclaimed. "Are you giving him enough milk?"

Mei Hwa's face flushed a deep red.

"Oh," the woman said, perceiving the problem. "You know, I have more than enough milk for my little ones. From now on, send your older boy to my house each day to pick up the extra milk."

The baby's mother couldn't believe her ears. Free milk! It was more than she could ask for. From then on Yun Foh had his regular supply of milk, and he grew stronger and chubbier by the day. A year later he had a baby brother. Together with their older brothers and sisters they grew up on the school campus. Although they were poor, life was pleasant for them in a Christian school environment.

In 1916 Sook Au and Mei Hwa once again packed their meager belongings for another move, this time to Meishan, where Sook Au had accepted a position teaching the Chinese language in a secondary school. Little Yun Foh's vision of the world, as well as the work of the Christian church, expanded. His eyes widened with surprise and wonder when with his family he stepped onto the school's huge compound.

"What's in all those buildings?" he asked his father.

Patiently Sook Au explained them one by one. "That huge one with the steeple is the church. And there's the elementary school, and just beyond it the high school. And see that other building? That's a school for blind people."

Yet it was in this exciting new community that tragedy struck once more.

One night Yun Foh heard loud moaning coming from the room of Siew Moi, the second of his older sisters. She rarely cried—in fact, she'd always been the one who comforted the other children. Always obedient and helpful, she was the joy and right arm of her mother. She not only ran errands and helped her mother with household chores, but was the one who made sure the younger children got fed, bandaged their wounds when they fell and hurt themselves, and herded them to the well in the evening for their baths.

Now that he'd come to think of it, Yun Foh had noticed a change in his sister. Lately she'd been stumbling around the house, clutching her abdomen while she tried to work. During the past couple days she hadn't gotten up at all, but had lain on her bed with her knees drawn up near her abdomen, extremely pale and whimpering with pain.

Mother had desperately tried everything to alleviate the discomfort—

heat pads and hot ointments—but the pain only increased. The doctor had given her a concoction of Chinese herbs, but it did no good.

Yun Foh was paralyzed with fear to hear her screaming all night long. Then just before dawn, a loud shriek pierced the air, followed by complete silence, eventually broken by a loud wailing. Lunging out of bed, he joined his brothers and sisters as they converged on Siew Moi's room. There they found Mother sobbing brokenheartedly over the still and pale form of her daughter. She had died of unknown causes, but as the family looked back later, they concluded that she had had a ruptured appendix.

For days Mother was prostrate with grief. But though she was inconsolable, life had to go on. Siew Moi, others told her, was safe in the arms of God, and now her other children needed her care.

The family's intimate encounter with death deeply affected the remaining siblings. The children gathered in a little council. "We've got to help Mother," they said. "How can we do this?"

"Let's study harder," one suggested.

"Right," another agreed, "so she won't have to pester us about it. And studying harder will help us forget our own grief. And we need to behave better."

"And," someone else added, "let's all take on the jobs that Siew Moi did."

But for Yun Foh the tragedy would affect him in more ways than one. As Mei Hwa continued to grieve, her husband thought of a practical way to alleviate his wife's sorrow. *What she needs,* he decided, *is a substitute for Siew Moi.*

Casting his eyes around the neighborhood, he soon made a decision. One of the daughters of a close friend had caught his eye. Petite, round-eyed, and with a flawless complexion, Tshin Chin impressed him as being a little girl who was hardworking and frugal—qualities that he valued. If anyone resembled Siew Moi, it was Tshin Chin.

As the idea grew in his mind, he approached his friend with his proposal. "With your permission, I would like to take Tshin Chin into my home to assuage my wife's grief, and with the plan of having her marry Yun Foh one day."

"I am delighted with your suggestion," his friend said. And before long Tshin Chin had joined the Chong family, helping to console Mei Hwa for the loss of Siew Moi.

4

Rendezvous at Au Mi San

A S THE TEACHER IN the Lutheran elementary school studied his class, he beamed fondly at his star pupil. "Yun Foh," he said, "you are a hardworking student."

Yun Foh lowered his head modestly. A couple nearby girls giggled.

"I wish every student were like you," the teacher continued, raising his voice. "Your parents must be proud to have you as a son."

Indeed, Mei Hwa and Sook Au burst with pride each time Yun Foh showed them his grade cards. "He's going to be a great scholar someday," they told each other. "And what's so nice is that he's one of our best-behaved children. Our other sons get into scrapes and fights—but Yun Foh never gives us any problems."

And what eased their minds even more was that the boy's two best friends were Chang Chi Kwan, the son of the church pastor, and Chen Sheng Cheng, the son of a wealthy businessman, both from solid Christian homes.

"After all," Mei Hwa said to her husband, "what can go wrong if Yun Foh is in the company of the pastor's boy?"

Little did she know.

One Sunday three small figures—Yun Foh and his friends Chi Kwan and Sheng Cheng—slipped onto the almost-deserted campus. Like the legendary Liu Bei, Zhang Fei and Guan Yu, characters in the Chinese legend of the three kingdoms, the three had formed a pact to be sworn brothers.

Unzipping their schoolbags, they quickly exchanged books and made a beeline for the water tower—their little hideaway where they could spend hours doing what they liked. The water tower was a tall wooden structure with a flat platform at the top that held the water tank. The platform had plenty of space left for the boys to sit on, their backs against the water tank.

Then came silence—hours of it. The only sound was the rustling of book pages.

To all appearance, the three adolescents were diligently studying their schoolbooks. All three were avid readers—but these were novels, not textbooks. After they had exhausted all the novels in the library, they'd hit on a convenient way to get as many others as they could lay hands on and yet save money—each would buy a novel, and when he was done with it, he'd pass it around to the others.

One day Chi Kwan opened a new novel and excitedly yelled, "Listen to me, guys! Do you want to be gods?"

Sheng Cheng's eyebrows knit together in puzzlement. "What?"

"Gods?" Yun Foh asked. "How?"

"Read this." Chi Kwan pushed the book at them. "It says that if you want to be transformed into a god, all you have to do is go to Au Mi San."

"You mean the mountain?"

"Right. In the Xichuan province."

"Let's do it!" all three exclaimed in unison. The vision of being gods flying through the air with magic swords, invincible and powerful, appealed to their imagination. They made up their minds to go to Au Mi San as soon as they could.

Secretly they began to lay plans. It would be a long and arduous journey that would take them through Guangdong and two other provinces. Even though they planned to travel by stages and walk most of the way, they needed money for food and lodging. Their young minds hadn't grasped the fact that Au Mi San was thousands of miles away!

In the days that followed, parents and friends were mystified to see the three boys scurrying around, trying to get all the odd jobs they could. Each had a little pig-shaped clay bank with a slot in the top, and into those slots they dropped all their earnings.

Then came the day they had waited for. Smuggling their pig banks out of their houses, they hurried to the water tower and cracked them open with trembling hands. Carefully they counted, their excitement growing by the minute, and their loud cheers almost gave the game away. Finally they had saved what they thought was enough money. Now they sat down to decide when they would leave.

September 28, 1924, was a Sunday. Not only did this day happen to be Confucius' birthday; it also coincided with a mysterious "illness" that afflicted each boy.

"Yun Foh," Mei Hwa called. "Time to get up for church."

No answer.

"That's funny," she said to her husband. "He's usually the first one up and ready to go. Yun Foh!"

She glanced through the door into his room. "He's still asleep," she said to her husband. "And his face looks flushed." Hurrying to his bedside, she put a worried hand on his forehead, which was curiously cool. She couldn't know, of course, that it wasn't fever but excitement and guilt she saw on his face.

Stirring, he opened his eyes.

"My poor little boy," she said comfortingly. "What's wrong with you? Why don't you just stay home and rest today?" He nodded. Later she remembered that the nod had seemed to come a bit too quickly.

Soon the family left for church, and silence reigned in the house. Once they had gone, Yun Foh dragged a bulging backpack from under his bed, shot out the door, and hurried to the water tower hideout. His two friends were already there.

Never having ventured out of the town before, the three boys were bursting with the excitement of traveling all on their own. The first half of the day slipped by quickly as they skipped along the path, chatting loudly and merrily. But by noon all three had begun to limp. Blisters had developed on feet unused to walking long distances.

"Ouch!" Yun Foh moaned. "I can't take another step! My feet are killing me."

"Be patient," Chi Kwan soothed. "Do you see what I do?" Ahead of them huddled a small town. Eagerly they hobbled on. A wave of homesickness swept over them as they passed through the village gates, even though nothing seemed familiar about it—even the animals looked different. Where would they spend the night? The dim lights of a small inn caught their attention. Without a word they tottered toward it and stumbled across its threshold.

The innkeeper peered over the counter and down at the three weary boys. "What do you want, kids?" he growled.

"A room for three, please," Chi Kwan said timidly.

The man's eyes narrowed. "Do you have money to pay for the room?"

They nodded.

"And where are your parents?"

No answer.

He glared. "Are you running away from home?"

Chi Kwan dug in his pocket. His fingers emerged, clutching a wad of money. "No problem," he lied confidently. "We've just been on an excursion, and we're too far away from home to get back tonight. So we thought we'd stay here and head home first thing in the morning."

The innkeeper stared at them hard for a moment more, then finally shrugged and gave them a room key. *Just to make sure,* he thought, *I'm going to keep an eye on these little rascals.*

That night in the darkness a small whimper escaped the lips of Yun Foh.

"What?" Chi Kwan's voice had a bit of a wobble in it.

Yun Foh turned over on the cold, hard bed. He dug his fist into his mouth to stifle the sobs that threatened to spill out. *I want to go home,* he thought with an aching heart. *Mom and Dad and my brothers are probably out frantically searching for me.* Filled with guilt and remorse, he was ready to forget all about his adventure to Au Mi San. *But there's no turning back,* he thought. *I can't face my brothers' scorn. I'd never live this down. No, come what may, I've got to go on.*

Arriving home from church, Mother had immediately gone into Yun Foh's room to check on him. All she saw was an empty, well-made bed.

"That's good," she said to the rest of the family. "He's recovered enough to go out and play. By now he's probably hungry and will be here for lunch."

But lunchtime came with no sign of the boy. As the afternoon wore on, the family still didn't worry much. Yun Foh had never been irresponsible—he must be with friends.

By suppertime and sundown, however, his parents had become alarmed. "Yun Mook," Dad said to his oldest son, "go check at Chi Kwan's house. Maybe your brother's there." When Yun Mook jogged over to the pastor's residence, to his surprise he found a brother of Sheng Cheng arriving on the same errand. Finally it dawned on all the parents that all three boys were missing.

Then the hunt began in earnest. Frantically the adults inquired at the homes of the boys' other classmates. None had seen them all day. They searched the village's play areas thoroughly.

"Check the village pond," someone suggested. "A lot of kids go there to play."

But the boys weren't there. Fear gripped the moms and dads. Had their boys drowned while playing in the water? The villagers formed an armada of little boats and dredged the pond for any bodies that might be floating below the surface of the muddy water.

"The schoolhouse," another parent exclaimed. "Let's check their desks. Maybe we'll find a clue there!" Hurrying to it, Chi Kwan's brother flipped open the top of his desk. "Look!" he shouted. "Here's a letter!"

There on top of his neat pile of books sat an envelope addressed to his parents. Pastor Chang tore open the envelope to discover a note in his son's neat handwriting:

> "Dear Parents and Family:
>
> "I believe that you must be really concerned over our sudden disappearance. Please don't worry about us. Actually the three of us have decided to go to Au Mi mountain in the Xichuan province to be deified.
>
> "We have not forgotten what our parents have done for us and plan to come home some time in the future—three to five years at the earliest and eight to 10 years at the longest. We will be back to see you as gods. Then we will be able to take good care of you. Goodbye till then.
>
> > "Sheng Cheng, Chi Kwan, and Yun Foh."

Mei Hwa's mouth had fallen as far open as it could. "That can't be true," she kept repeating in a dazed voice. "I can't believe it. There's some mistake. Yun Foh would never run away from home. He's too—too *timid.*"

But teachers and parents were already busy organizing search parties.

"Let's get going," someone said urgently. "We've got to track down those boys before they get too far."

"Right," someone else added. "And before they fall into the hands of mountain bandits." So the various search parties went their separate ways, scouring the village commons, then fanning out to nearby towns to check the shops.

5

Student Radical

THE FOLLOWING MORNING at the crack of dawn the three vagabonds got up to continue their journey. Yun Foh hadn't slept a wink, and his eyes were red and swollen from crying.

Still suspicious, the innkeeper grilled them once more, but again the glib Chi Kwan managed to explain their presence. They hurried away from the inn. But it was pouring rain by the time they reached the next town. Soaked to their skin, they dragged themselves into the first inn they could find and slept there for the night.

"Look!" Chi Kwan exclaimed in dismay the next morning. "The rain is coming down in sheets, and we don't have any umbrellas. Looks as if we'll have to spend another day here."

The day crept by. Since they'd lost a day's travel, they made it a point to get up extra early the next morning. Sleepily gulping down their breakfast, they started toward the door.

Chi Kwan was in the lead. Suddenly he stopped midstep, then shrank back into the shadows, bumping into the other boys. "Look!" he hissed. "Isn't that Mr. Ching Sui?"

Too late! Mr. Ching Sui, their teacher, loomed in the doorway and fixed them with a piercing gaze.

"Wh—wh—what are you doing here, Mr. Ching?" the boys stammered.

"That's not the point," the man countered. "What are *you* doing here?"

Silently they stared at the floor.

"So you have no answer?" he asked sternly. "Well, your parents have sent me to bring you home. Here, give me all of your luggage and come home with me immediately."

With their luggage confiscated, the boys had no choice but to accompany him. But they secretly vowed that they would bide their time and wait for another opportunity to continue their journey to Au Mi San.

Two days later they walked sheepishly onto the school campus. At that moment the rest of the students were at chapel in the assembly hall, and they broke into cheers at the sight of the boys. Then they burst into song—one they'd especially composed to welcome them home.

Actually, deep in their hearts, the three were glad to be back. From then on, all the parents and teachers took special pains to monitor the activities of the boys under their care, and to instruct them on the folly of believing everything they read in storybooks.

An account of the boys' escapade reached Shanghai and appeared in the local newspaper. As for Yun Foh, he got into no more scrapes until he went off as a boarding student to Lock Yoke High School, one of the most prestigious schools operated by the Lutheran Church in Meishan.

During Yun Foh's high school years a growing tension filled the air in China. Whenever he left Lock Yoke's campus and walked the downtown streets, he saw many foreigners in khaki uniforms. As he read the newspaper and listened to conversations around him, the word "Japanese" kept popping up. At school his teachers appeared troubled and apprehensive.

Why are people so hostile to the Japanese? Yun Foh wondered at first. But soon he began to understand the fear and tension. The khaki uniforms belonged to tight-lipped Japanese soldiers, and China was under the threat of their occupation. Each day the newspapers carried reports of northern regions that had fallen under Japanese domination, with key Chinese leaders being arrested.

News of these strange, unsettling events drifted into the school, and the students had strict orders not to leave campus without permission. However, one day Yun Foh's curiosity got the better of him. Together with his younger brother and a few other students, he slipped off campus and into town.

At first, everything seemed normal. Then all of a sudden they heard the *tramp-tramp-tramp* of marching feet. Yun Foh and his group rounded a corner, expecting to see soldiers, but instead they saw a horde of young students in school uniforms just like theirs. Waving high the Chinese flag, the students uttered a rhythmic battle cry: "Down with the Japanese! Long live China! Down with the Japanese! Long live China!"

"Look!" one of Yun Foh's fellow students exclaimed. "The whole street is on fire!" Sure enough, huge bonfires lit all along the avenue made it look as though the city was aflame.

"Why are they looting the shops?" a puzzled Yun Foh asked. Indeed, as the students marched down the street, they broke into stores and emerged with loads of merchandise in their arms, which they then threw into the bonfires.

"Japanese goods," one of Yun Foh's friends explained, examining them closely. "They're protesting against the Japanese presence."

Suddenly the police arrived, and rifle shots crackled through the air. The students scattered in different directions, only to regroup farther down the street. It happened again and again, until some of them found themselves struggling in the grip of the police. Terrified, Yun Foh and his friends fled back to the safety of the campus.

Although he and his friends didn't take part in the big demonstrations downtown, what they'd witnessed did affect them. The militant, restless conditions penetrated the atmosphere of the school campus, and a rebellious spirit surfaced, creating student dissatisfaction and demands for reform. They even formed student unions, and Yun Foh soon found himself embroiled in something of a campus protest.

Although he usually enjoyed attending class, one morning he found himself dragging his feet. Bleary-eyed, he'd spent most of the previous night struggling with his math problems, and by dawn he felt no more confident about them.

I hate this class, he fumed silently. *I can't understand it, and Pastor Mei's feeble attempts to explain the problems only confuse me more. Worst of all, the final exam is getting closer and closer.*

He walked into the classroom to find a group of agitated fellow students clustered in heated discussion. "We must go see the principal!" one exclaimed angrily. "I have had enough of this!"

"Pastor Mei may be a good pastor," another added, "but he's a lousy math teacher. I don't understand a thing he says."

"You're right," the others agreed, "Let's do it—right now. If we don't demand a new teacher, we'll all fail the finals."

Yun Foh hesitated. "Wait a minute," he said. "This is going to be a real blow to Pastor Mei's ego. Isn't there some other way to deal with this?"

"Like what?" someone demanded.

"I mean, doesn't the Bible talk about showing respect to our elders and people in authority?"

"You're a coward," another student sneered.

"No, I'm not. It's just that this is a really drastic step for Christian students to take."

"You're just chicken," the other said flatly. "Don't worry. You don't have to go with us if you don't want to."

In spite of his protests, Yun Foh found a struggle taking place in his heart. Even though he couldn't bear to show disrespect to his teacher, he firmly believed that he and his friends needed better instruction.

"Chicken! Chicken!" the others began chanting.

Suddenly Yun Foh's lips tightened. *I'm no chicken. I'll show them I'm not afraid.* "I'm with you," he said aloud. "Let's go."

As one they marched to the principal's office, demanded an audience, and pushed their way in. Everyone spoke at once.

"We want a new math teacher!"

"Pastor Mei is no math teacher! We can't understand anything he says!"

"We are going to fail the finals!"

The principal finally got to his feet and waved his arms. "Wait! Wait!" he commanded. "One person at a time."

"All right. Calm down now," he said after he'd listened to their complaints. "Just go back to class. I promise that I'll look into the matter."

Taking him at his word, the students waited patiently. But each day as they walked into the classroom, there stood Pastor Mei. The final exam was just a frighteningly short time away, and they tried unsuccessfully to get another audience with the principal. Finally they again decided to make their needs dramatically known.

The day for the math examination arrived. Walking into his classroom, Pastor Mei discovered that all the desks were empty—not a student was in sight.

Strange! he thought to himself. *Where is everybody? Have they gotten the examination schedule mixed up?* Although he waited, no one turned up, not even Yun Foh.

"My class has boycotted my exam!" he whispered to himself, then hurried to the principal to report.

The school administration immediately decided to take disciplinary action. It summoned all the student leaders to the principal's office.

"Finally our protest has registered," they told each other. "Now we'll get some action!" Wearing a look of triumphant defiance, they marched into his office.

"You must apologize to Pastor Mei," the principal demanded, "and also to the school, for your act of defiance."

The furious students, emerging from his office a few minutes later, huddled in the hall. "We *can't* apologize," they growled. "So we *won't*."

The administration responded by expelling the student leaders from school. Still defiant, the rest of the student body protested their leaders' expulsion and continued to agitate for a new teacher. The school refused to budge. In protest, many left to attend other schools but continued to agitate, demonstrating on a larger scale outside the school grounds and in other nearby areas.

In those days, however, the word of the teachers and the administration was law. The institution refused to concede to the students' demands, and continued to retain Pastor Mei's services. The students reported the matter to county officials, but the local government backed the school administration and ordered student leaders to stop the unrest and concentrate on their studies.

For Yun Foh, this unpleasant experience would return to haunt him years later. While attending college, he and a fellow student sold books door to door during a summer break. To his chagrin, he discovered that the pastor of the church in his assigned territory was none other than his old math teacher, Pastor Mei, who'd been embarrassed by the student protest and had gone back to pastoring.

To keep expenses down, Yun Foh and his partner had to sleep in the church building. Still smarting from the emotional wounds inflicted on him so many years ago, Pastor Mei received them with extreme coldness.

Yun Foh took the first chance possible to try to explain that he was a reluctant participant in the protest. However, nothing could convince the pastor of his innocence. Unpleasant as it was, this experience taught Yun

Foh to be more sensitive to the feelings of others and not to take part in anything that would hurt another individual, no matter how just the cause. This lesson would serve him well as he worked as a pastor and an administrator later on in life.

6

From Death's Shadow
to Greater Light

OUCH! *OHHHHHH!"*

Yun Foh jerked awake in the darkness. For a split second he didn't know why he'd awakened, but then pain flooded over him. His entire abdomen twisted with terrible stomach cramps. Tumbling from his bed, he ran to the restroom with a horrendous case of diarrhea.

"Go away," he whispered fiercely, head between his knees, to whatever ailed him. "It's my last semester at Lock Yoke High School, and *I cannot get sick."*

But the illness did not leave. In the days that followed, Yun Foh saw doctor after doctor. For a while he'd get better, only to suffer a severe relapse, which left him so weak that often one of his seven roommates, or even his younger brother, had to carry him to his classrooms and elsewhere. However, raw determination brought him through, and he managed to graduate.

When he returned home, his father took things in hand. "Don't worry; we'll get you better. We'll take you to Chinese doctors and get you Chinese medicine. And if that doesn't work, we'll see Western doctors about Western medicine."

But nothing helped. His health continued to slide downhill.

Why is God doing this to me? he asked himself. *Or if He's not doing it, then why is He allowing it? I've done my best to get top grades. I'm well known for my good conduct. Except for that math class protest, I've taken great pains to obey all the regulations. And I've even attended all the school's religious meetings.*

My one big dream is to go on to college or university in China or even Germany. Now it's all going to collapse into nothing!

And still the debilitating illness clung tenaciously to him. He was getting weaker by the day, and sometimes he was so depressed and hopeless that death seemed to stare directly into his face.

Then one day, when he seemed to be at the absolute end of his rope, hope came from an unexpected quarter.

"Come, Yun Foh, get dressed," Mother said, hurrying into his room with shining eyes. "Come with me."

"Where to?" Yun Foh groaned. "Another doctor?"

"Not a doctor."

Her son's face crumpled in pain. "I'm not going anywhere. I can hardly lift myself out of bed."

"Don't worry," she said soothingly. "I've asked your brother to help get you there."

Yun Foh crawled painfully out of bed and dressed with real effort. "Where are you taking me this time?"

"We are going to a revival meeting."

Her son sagged wearily. "Mom," he said feebly, with as much spirit as he could muster, "why are you dragging me to a religious meeting? I can't even sit up straight in a chair without getting sick." And though he didn't say it aloud, he thought, *What's the use? My prayers for healing don't seem to have gone beyond the ceiling.*

"Oh," Mother assured him, "this meeting is quite different from the rest."

"I doubt it," he moaned.

"You will see," she insisted. "The church in Guangzhou has sent a team of people to our town to conduct revival meetings and do faith healing. These people are able to heal the sick through prayer. Many church members have gone to the meetings and regained their health. This may be your one and only chance."

He opened his mouth to protest again, but found he had no strength. It was easier simply to let his mother and brother pull him to his feet. Staggering weak-kneed between them, he finally reached the meeting place.

Then something amazing happened. Yun Foh found that he was able to sit up straight, and for the rest of the evening he sat enthralled as the Lutheran evangelistic team delivered a powerful message regarding the divine Healer. Then they began to pray for sick people, and a good number were healed and immediately gave moving testimonies about their experiences. Many church members confessed their sins and repented. Even unchurched people gave their hearts to God.

Though Yun Foh himself didn't experience immediate healing, from then on he found himself drawn irresistibly to the meetings. To this point he'd been merely a nominal Christian. But now he felt God's Spirit leading him to a real conversion experience. For the first time since joining a Christian church, he began to study his Bible and pray for God to heal him and to show him the direction his life should take.

During one of the revival meetings Yun Foh first heard about Seventh-day Adventists. One evening a member of the evangelistic team related a dream he'd had about a local Adventist pastor. "This man," the speaker said, "is a very sincere evangelist."

When word reached the Adventist pastor, he began attending the revival meetings in the Lutheran church and participated in its activities.

A discussion the members of the Lutheran church had one day caught Yun Foh's attention. "Those Adventists are a queer sect," one of them said. "They observe the Jewish Sabbath, and what's more, they don't eat certain kinds of meat, like pork."

That's so sad, Yun Foh thought to himself. *Why on earth do these poor people still keep the Jews' Sabbath? Don't they know they're observing the wrong day? I'll just have to go straighten them out.*

Although he didn't have the church's address, he knew its general direction. So one day he set out—but got lost on the way.

"Sir," he asked the first person who came along, "can you tell me where the Seventh-day Adventist church is?"

"And why are you looking for the Adventist church, young man?" the stranger asked.

"I have some questions I need to ask the pastor."

"You do?" The man grinned. "You might as well come along with me—because I'm the pastor you're looking for."

"But I don't recognize you," Yun Foh said. "I know the Adventist pastor."

"He got transferred not too long ago. I'm his replacement."

Surely it is providential, Yun Foh thought, *that I have run into the pastor himself!*

Once they arrived at the church, the young man bombarded Pastor Young Tau Yoong and his two helpers with general questions about the church, and kept them busy answering them the rest of the day. However, as he fired question after question, Yun Foh discovered himself changing from a bringer of truth to a receiver. At each new Bible concept that the Adventist men explained to him, his eyes lit up with excitement.

Then the topic of the Sabbath came up.

"Did you know," the pastor asked, "that the seventh-day Sabbath was instituted at Creation and was observed by Adam and Eve?"

"Of course," Yun Foh shot back. "The Bible does say that the Sabbath is the seventh day. But why are you worshipping on Saturday instead of Sunday?"

The pastor blinked. "That's precisely the point. Saturday is the seventh-day Sabbath we're talking about."

"I can't believe it. You're not counting correctly."

"Here's a calendar," the pastor said, walking to his office wall. "Look— one, two three, four, five, six, seven. Saturday's the seventh day."

When it came time for the dazed young man to leave, the pastor loaded him down with several books by Ellen White, as well as some tracts and church magazines.

Tucking the books under his arms, Yun Foh hurried home and plunged right into them, reading far into the night. Before the end of the week he had become a strong believer in Ellen White's messages, especially the ones that spoke about the Sabbath. What especially gripped him was her account of a dream in which she saw God's Ten Commandments, with the fourth one encircled by a light.

Yun Foh couldn't wait to share his discoveries with his family members, and to his delight they were receptive to them.

Next he turned his efforts toward his fellow Lutheran church members. *My friends are already Christians,* he told himself. *They believe the Bible. Before long they'll be converted to the Sabbath truth.* He had visions of his whole congregation joining the Adventist faith—which would mean that another entire Adventist church would be born!

He was totally unprepared, however, for the stiff resistance and even hostility he encountered. The church members he spoke to used every possible argument to dissuade him from believing what he had read.

43

When they couldn't shake his belief, one prominent member said, "Look, Yun Foh, the day we worship on doesn't make any difference—the important thing is our devotion to God."

"But—" Yun Foh protested.

"And as to Mrs. Ellen White," the man continued, "I'm going to lend you some books that will give you the real truth about her, and also about this denomination that has you in its clutches."

Young and inexperienced, Yun Foh found himself totally lost in a maze of conflicting ideas. He found his belief in the Adventist faith derailed by what appeared to be convincing arguments from his church's members and the books they lent him.

"I've had enough of this," he finally muttered. "My brains feel scrambled. I'm going to set aside every other book, and work this matter through with the Bible alone." And so, praying for divine guidance, he began to study the Word. As he did so, the Spirit of God continued to work within him, giving him no rest.

One day while reading in the Gospels, he made a life-changing decision.

It says here that Jesus spent several nights in prayer, he thought to himself. *And it seems as though He did this especially before He made major decisions. I'm going to try that.*

So Yun Foh climbed the high mountain near his home and spent the entire night there, meditating on all that he had read in the Bible and praying for God to help him make the right decision about his spiritual future.

"That was my 'Jacob experience at Jabbok,'" he would later say. "At dawn my mind was made up." And down the mountain he came.

"I want to let you know," he told the family, "that on this very Saturday I am going to start attending the Adventist church."

"Then we will go with you," they said, delighting him immensely. And when Sabbath came, the entire family of 13 filed into the Seventh-day Adventist church.

Needless to say, the Adventist pastor was also overjoyed and deeply moved. From then on the family observed the Sabbath. But ties with the Lutheran Church, which stretched back to when his father had first encountered Christianity, could not be severed suddenly. Both Father and Yun Foh's older brothers had worked in institutions operated by that denomination for most of their working life. Moreover, Yun Foh and his siblings had studied in Lutheran schools. Their departure from it, the parents decided, had to be slow and gradual, so they continued to attend both churches until the time came for them to cut any ties with Lutheranism completely.

Yun Foh's eventual decision to be baptized into the Adventist Church bore testimony to the faith and foresight of the local church leaders. In 1928—even though he had not yet been baptized—they sent him as a delegate to the annual council of the local Hakka Mission.

He met many Adventist pastors, administrators, union leaders, and church employees and listened to such great speakers as Pastor Frederick Lee, a veteran China missionary and father of Milton Lee. During the meeting Yun Foh made his commitment to be baptized. And on December 7, 1928, right there at the Hakka Mission council, encircled by the 39 other young people baptized together with him, he rose from the river to the strains of "I Surrender All." And though his journey to the Seventh-day Adventist Church had been a long, difficult, circuitous, and sometimes painful route, his heart was finally at peace.

In 1898, 7-year-old Mei Hwa was brought here to the Chong family home as a child bride. None of the original dwellings are left (the photo is recent), but the rice paddy field is still in the foreground, and the hill ascending to the right is where Yun Foh later had his "Jabbok experience," in which he made his decision to join the Seventh-day Adventist Church.

7

In Training for the Master's Service

A YEAR AFTER HIS BAPTISM Yun Foh again went as a delegate to the Hakka Mission annual council. Only this time (though a relatively inexperienced youth) he found himself nominated to be the mission's literature evangelism director. But the mission suddenly overruled it.

"No," one leader said firmly, "we're going to grant Yun Foh a year's scholarship to the San Yü Training Institute. This young man needs to become a pastor."

Bewildered but delighted (and encouraged by his father's blessing), Yun Foh embarked on the long, complicated train journey. He'd never traveled such great distances before, yet the Lord sent him help in the form of a young man he met in a hotel. His companion shepherded him about, helping him buy tickets and personally seeing him off at the railway station.

"The college campus, overlooking the renowned Yangtze River and located about 160 miles from Shanghai and 30 miles from Nanjing, was beautiful," Yun Foh would recall later. "The campus had seven hills—like Rome! And each of the major buildings stood on its own hill. The school also had a water tower with two tanks, which was where I went to pray and meditate and think about God.

"One of the main reasons I was so proud of our campus was that it was a model of excellent agriculture. The farm had several new pieces of machinery that the villagers had never seen before. It was fun to watch them standing at the edge of the field gawking! I'd never eaten a strawberry before, or even seen one. Yet they grew them on campus—huge, juicy ones.

"People told an amazing story about how the Lord had blessed the college because of tithing. Some time back a swarm of locusts had swept over the area. The president and the faculty prayed and reminded God of His promises to those who are faithful in returning to Him what is His. Just as the locusts reached the edge of the campus fields, they changed direction!

"The villagers would always argue among themselves about why the college hens laid so many eggs and theirs didn't. Again and again we heard stories of how the agricultural program was a powerful witness to God's ways."

San Yü College was blessed with excellent faculty—both Chinese and Americans. President Denton E. Rebok was the one who'd discovered this beautiful campus and who'd found resourceful ways to provide the farm with its equipment. Under his leadership the college expanded to become one of China's most renowned educational centers.

Yun Foh devoured the subjects he took. He treasured not only each moment in class but also the close friendships he formed on campus, both the young men and the young women. It was in times like these, though, when he felt trapped in the cross-cultural conflict typical of people exposed to a culture different from their own.

The foreign missionaries, not realizing what they were doing, encouraged young men and women to date and to relish the freedom of choosing their own life partners. Like some of his college mates, Yun Foh's parents had already selected his future wife. It was a unique struggle, yet even though at times he was tempted to take his friendship with some of the eligible women on campus further, he would remind himself: *I'm bound to a prearranged marriage, so I must not date anyone here. I have a fiancée waiting for me at home.* His dedication and devotion to God and the church impressed many of his fellow female students. They would have been delighted to marry him if he'd been free, yet they recognized his commitment to Tshin Chin and refrained from trying to pursue any intimate friendship with him.

In spite of such distractions, the first year flew by, and Yun Foh threw himself into summer literature evangelism work. However, he failed to earn enough money to pay for the next year. Sadly, he returned home to think out a plan of action, heart aching with longing—and a bit of resentment. Yet later, as he looked back, he would come to understand why God permitted the depressing experience. Like Moses in the wilderness,

47

the young man needed a long detour to gain the practical experiences he'd require for his future calling.

His first pastorate, in 1931, was at Yuan Shian. Though he earned only $18 a month, he not only tithed faithfully but also paid his younger brother's tuition. His poor but generous church members often shared vegetables from their own gardens with their struggling young pastor. But during those years he had the joyous privilege of baptizing his oldest brother and several other relatives.

Still, he felt his lack of education.

"Lord," he prayed desperately, "you know I've had only a year of college, and I've never even interned under a senior pastor. Please help me!"

One Sabbath a veteran Methodist minister visited Yun Foh's congregation.

"Do you mind," the older man asked, "if I attend here on Saturdays?"

"Not at all," Yun Foh said.

The two soon developed a close friendship, and the young pastor realized he had discovered a trustworthy mentor. The older man helped teach Sabbath school classes, and in return, Yun Foh attended the Sunday church and taught Sunday school classes. The two visited their members together, and even conducted evangelistic meetings. Yun Foh would later value these experiences immensely—they gave him a refreshing openness to doctrinal differences and prepared him to act as a mediator between denominations when misunderstandings arose.

At his next two appointments he served as both church pastor and school principal, which prepared him for later responsibilities in Kuching, Sarawak, and Singapore. In 1935 the mission sent him back to San Yü College—not for ministerial training, but for a year of industrial arts study, so he could return to train young people in the various trades. Stepping through the college portals, he once again plunged enthusiastically into the classwork: drafting, physics, chemistry, woodworking, and agriculture. The latter especially interested him, though he wondered sometimes what a pastor and school administrator would need with farm training. A few years later he would discover again that a far-seeing God knows how best to prepare His willing servants.

Determined to finish his college program, Yun Foh sold books during the summer, then received a position as assistant to the dormitory dean on campus to make up his final tuition needs. "I was back in school," he recalled later, "and now I was old enough to enjoy it even more! Dr. Rebok and Pastor A. A. Esteb delivered their sermons in fluent, cultured Chinese. They moved the students to tears during the annual Week of Prayer, and we saw great revivals. One time the students went to their rooms and brought out all questionable reading materials and burned them in bonfires.

"And then they became part of evangelistic support teams. Once their preaching so moved the villagers that they invited the team into their houses to collect all their idols, take them to the fire, and burn them. Seventeen people were baptized in the river as a result!"

Sadly, the ugly snout of war thrust itself into Chinese life. Back in 1931 Japan had invaded northeastern China (the Manchurian region), and tension between the two nations had escalated ever since. During 1937 a military clash at the Marco Polo Bridge near Beijing erupted into the Second Sino-Japanese War. Within months the Japanese had captured the national capital.

Toward the end of 1938 the Seventh-day Adventist denomination implemented a plan to offer humanitarian aid. "I took part in a high school and elementary teachers' retreat on campus," Yun Foh would relate years afterward. "After the Red Cross trained us, they organized us into a rescue brigade. I was put in charge of one of the teams, and we walked 40 miles to the Jiangshu Hospital. The Japanese air force had already started bombing in our area, and we had to get right to work. I still shudder at the memory of seeing a Japanese plane shot down. We had to go and pull the dead bodies out. It was gruesome!"

Because of the escalating battles, the college decided to close until the situation would improve. "You have a choice," its administrators told the students. "You can stay and work with the rescue teams, or return home."

Yun Foh decided to go home.

Rushing to the railway station, he found it a milling mass of refugees. Everybody had something strapped to his or her back or slung over the shoulder—backpacks, bawling babies, even howling animals. Each time a train screeched to a halt at the platform, the crowd surged forward and fought to get into the cars.

Fortunately, Yun Foh was so tightly wedged between the mass of people that their momentum carried him forward onto one of the coaches.

Others who failed to get in clambered onto the roofs of the cars and hung on for dear life.

I'm going to die of suffocation, Yun Foh thought desperately. *Lord, please help me. Help all of us!*

"But that was the least of our worries," he told his family later. "Normally this trip would have taken us a day and a night, but the train had to go slowly to keep from spilling people off the roof. So the journey stretched into three days and four nights! Every once in a while the engineers would spot Japanese bombers coming, or simply hear air-raid sirens. They'd bring the train to a halt, and all the passengers would jump off and get as far away as they could. Sometimes the bombers would hit the tracks, so we'd have to wait there until the railroad crews fixed them. Then there'd be this mad scramble back onto the coaches."

How thankful he was to finally arrive at Guangzhou without any broken bones.

"That's it," he said to himself. "I've had enough trauma to last a lifetime." Changing his travel plans, he hopped a train for Hong Kong, and quickly discovered that many of the China Division personnel, as well as those of the Shanghai Adventist Hospital and the denominational publishing house, had had the same idea. Once in Hong Kong, he found a job at the Signs of the Times Publishing House. A month later he was again on his way home to join the mobile evangelistic team working in the Hakka area.

8

Missionary to the Land of the Headhunters

Note to the reader: Like many other Christians of their era, Yun Foh and his new bride, Tshin Chin, decided to adopt Western first names when they traveled to foreign countries to work for the church.

ON APRIL 4, 1938, ITS GANGPLANK raised and its huge horn blasting mournfully, the Italian ocean liner slowly pulled away from the dock in Hong Kong's harbor. Joshua and Eunice (the names Yun Foh and his new bride, Tshin Chin, had chosen for mission service) stood on the deck, straining to catch a last glimpse of their homeland.

Eunice forlornly watched the other passengers. "Look," she said, "they're all holding paper streamers, and their loved ones are holding the other end. There's nobody to see us off." Suddenly she burst into tears. The two newlyweds had bidden parents, relatives, and friends farewell in their home village and in Guangzhou before coming to Hong Kong to catch the ocean liner that would take them to Borneo by way of Singapore.

"I know," Joshua said, swallowing a lump in his throat again and again. "But God is here. And He's not on the shore—He's going with us."

His arm around her shoulder, he too felt waves of homesickness wash over him—and also misgivings. As he pressed his lips to Eunice's hair, he thought back over the circumstances and events that had led up to this day.

At the height of the Sino-Japanese War he'd fled to Hong Kong. But when he finally returned home to the mainland, a telegram had arrived from Allen L. Ham, superintendent of the South China Union.

"Come immediately back to Hong Kong," it read, "as soon as you can make the trip."

What could he be summoning me for? Joshua had asked himself anxiously as he packed a suitcase. *I've done nothing wrong—as far as I know. What's the matter?*

One by one, he ticked off on his fingers some possible issues. *I've done my work faithfully. I've been proper in my conduct, not only with my church members but with my fiancée.* Eunice had been taking the nursing program at a school in the neighboring province.

Needless to say, his worries made the trip back to Hong Kong less than pleasant. Finally, heart palpitating, he presented himself at the office of the superintendent. The fact that the leader was wearing a warm smile somewhat relieved him.

"Come in, Joshua," the man said. "I want to congratulate you! We have received a request for a missionary to Kuching, and we've decided that you are the best candidate."

Joshua looked puzzled. "Kuching?"

"In Sarawak."

"Where on earth is that?"

"Don't you know Sarawak? It's a state in Borneo, one of the islands in the South China Sea."

Feeling his cheeks going numb, Joshua stuttered, "But . . . but . . . I'm happy where I am, Elder Ham."

The administrator just smiled.

Joshua tried again. "I don't know a single person overseas," he stammered. "And I don't really *need* to go anywhere."

"You're the right person for this mission assignment, Joshua," Ham said intently. "Please tell me yes."

Swallowing, Joshua looked desperately around the office, as if seeking strength. "Elder Ham," he finally said, "this is a surprise to me. I'm totally perplexed as to what to do."

"I can understand that."

"May I please have some time to think things over? I'd like to seek counsel from my family and friends."

Reluctantly Elder Ham nodded. "Certainly. But please pray and seek counsel quickly. We desperately need to fill this position, and we believe you're the man for it. Let me know as soon as you can."

In the days that followed, Joshua felt like a piece of hamburger meat sandwiched between two very different schools of thought. First he broke the news to a close friend teaching in a Hong Kong secondary school.

Eyes intent, a solemn Joshua seems to be peering into an uncertain but adventurous future as he begins his first foreign mission assignment: pastor and schoolteacher in Kuching, Borneo

"No, *no*," his friend said. "This is not a good time for you to leave. If I were you, I'd stay close to home. Your parents aren't getting any younger—and your father's ill. It's your responsibility to help care for them. At this time in their lives they need you more than ever. Let someone else go to Borneo."

"Well—" Joshua began, but his friend cut him off.

"Isn't it your first responsibility to work for the Chinese people rather than for people of a foreign land?"

"I've got a brother who could take care of my parents," Joshua said doubtfully.

"And one more thing," the friend said, tapping Joshua on the chest. "Haven't you heard that Borneo is the land of headhunters? You'll be risking your neck—literally!"

Now more perplexed than ever, Joshua decided to travel to the nursing school Eunice attended. *I wonder how she'll take this,* he mused. *She still has several months before she graduates. And we hadn't planned to get married until we'd both worked a year.*

"Joshua's downstairs?" Eunice gasped when she heard of his arrival. As she left her room she chirped over her shoulder to her roommate, "Maybe he's brought some good news from home."

Tripping lightly down the stairs with a joyful smile, she was surprised to see a serious look on her betrothed's face.

"Eunice, may we talk? Somewhere in private?" And in a quiet room just off the main lobby he dropped his bombshell on her.

Even though he knew he was bringing startling news, her dramatic response still floored him. When they were both children, his parents had selected this sweet-faced girl with smiling eyes and flawless complexion as his future wife, and as a rule she was docile, quiet, and compliant. Up to this point she'd always looked up to him and agreed with all his decisions.

Now her face went numb with shock. For what seemed like five minutes she remained speechless. Then tears—and rebellion—welled up in her gaze. Her hands shook as she dabbed her eyes.

"Where? When?" she asked in a thick voice. "Have you actually promised to go?"

He opened his mouth, but quickly closed it again as a sudden torrent of words poured from her trembling lips. "You can't be serious! I haven't even graduated, and after that I want to start my career! You'll ruin it all for me!"

"Eunice—"

"And what would I do without all my friends?" she quavered.

Her thoughts turned to Cecil, a young man training to be a radiologist. He had been in hot pursuit of her, but she had properly refrained from accepting his dates since she was already betrothed to Joshua. But secretly she enjoyed Cecil's attention.

Cecil is more like the romantic heroes I read about in books, she thought. *With Joshua it's different. I've grown up alongside him. He's more like a brother than a fiancé. And now he wants to drag me away to some unheard-of place.*

Clearing his throat, he tried again. "Eunice, my darling—"

"What am I going to do in a strange land?" she wailed. "I don't even know where Borneo *is.*"

Then she burst into tears again and sobbed for a long time. It tore at Joshua's heart and sent him reeling from the school campus.

When he traveled to his parents' home and broke the news to his mother, it was no more encouraging.

"No, Yun Foh, not this! Not this!" she whispered in a heartbroken voice. "You're my favorite son. You can't go at this time. What would we do without you? Your father's health is failing fast. Go look at him, there in his room lying on his bed. You'll see for yourself that he won't last much longer. Ah, my son, don't you think he will want to have all his children around him when he passes to his rest?"

Joshua squeezed his eyes shut so she wouldn't see his tears.

"You know how much I worry about you," she reminded him. "I would worry about you if you were only two provinces away from me. Now you tell me you're going to spend many days on the ocean in a little steamer, and you'll end up in a land I've never even heard of before. All around you will be dark-skinned people. What would you ever want," she asked sharply, "with people who *can't even speak Chinese?*"

But when Joshua entered his father's bedroom, it was like finding calm shelter in the midst of a storm. The older man encouraged him to go along with the needs of the church.

"That's what I did with the Lutherans," he reminded his son. "Keep in mind what the Adventists have done for you. They've provided you with an excellent college education, and they've given you opportunities to work."

"But what about you? You're not well."

His father shook his head impatiently. "What is more satisfying," he demanded, "than doing the will of God?" He glanced at the door. "Don't let your mother tempt you away from this opportunity. And by all means, don't let concerns about my health stand in your way when it comes to accepting this call. Do you understand?"

"But I would feel so guilty if I went away and if you—" Joshua paused, a lump in his throat.

"Let's allow God to take care of me and the rest of your loved ones," the older man commanded. With difficulty he raised himself on one elbow and looked his son straight in the eye. "I would be very proud to have my son go as a missionary from China to another land. Here, let me walk with you to the door."

Despite his son's protests, the father got painfully out of bed and insisted on grasping a walking stick and accompanying him to the front door to say farewell. Though Joshua was truly thankful for his father's encouragement, forever etched in his memory would be the picture of the frail, weak figure leaning on the walking stick. And each time he relived that scene, he felt afresh the pain that had stabbed his heart when he waved goodbye to his father, knowing that he might never see him again.

And now Joshua's internal battle really began.

"God," he cried out in anguish. "What should I do? You know I want Your will in my life. But—but I can't ignore the needs of my family and my people. And my future wife has her doubts as well."

During the next few days he could neither eat nor sleep normally. When, after tossing and turning on his bed, he did manage to drift off, he had nightmares in which screaming, half-naked natives wielding parangs (machetes) chased him, threatening to slice off his head.

He found himself longing for someone else to make the decision. But he was the one who would have to decide. And after a week of painful deliberation, he traveled back to the president's office more bewildered than ever.

"I can see the struggle you're going through," Superintendent Ham told him kindly. "But I encourage you to remember how good God has been to you. I believe it's in His plan that, as a dedicated worker in His church, you should accept the decision of its leadership. You know," he said thoughtfully, "many of the foreign missionaries who've come to China have gone through your same experience. They've submitted themselves to the will of God, and have allowed Him to send them—at the decision of their leaders—to areas where the church needed their service."

Joshua gave a trembling sigh and nodded.

"These missionaries have sacrificed family and friends to bring the gospel to the Chinese people," Elder Ham continued. "Don't you think it's now your responsibility to carry the message still further?"

The younger man said nothing.

"Let's pray about it together," the mission leader finally said. And as the two knelt to plead for divine guidance, Joshua made his decision. "Dear heavenly Father," he prayed. "Regardless of any personal sacrifice I have to make, I will accept Your call."

Then began the hectic rounds of going to the immigration office—and preparing for his wedding. "You'd better take along a wife," A. L. Ham had insisted. "It's unthinkable for you to go as a missionary pastor if you're single."

So on March 1, 1938, Joshua and Eunice married in a simple ceremony at the Fuizhou church. All their relatives and friends came to Guangzhou to attend the wedding, and Pastor J. P. Anderson, former president of the Hakka Mission, officiated.

Joshua's fiancée, Eunice, was a child bride like Mei Hwa, brought into the Chong home to grow up with her future husband. This photo was taken about the time Joshua visited her with the news that he'd been called to mission service, and they needed to be married immediately!

Joshua felt a tugging on his sleeve.

He blinked, shook his head, and blinked again. No, he was not in his wedding suit listening to Pastor Anderson's vows, but on the vibrating deck of an ocean liner. Staring around him, he discovered that the ship had almost cleared Hong Kong's harbor and was heading out to open sea.

"Come on," Eunice said, tugging again. "Let's go inside. I'm cold."

Together they went below deck to weather out the rough seas ahead. For four days the ship's rocking and rolling glued them to their bed with seasickness. On the occasions when they did manage to stagger on to the deck for a breath of fresh air, the sight of the foaming sea and never-ending horizon merely intensified their homesickness and increased their misgivings.

9

Sarawak

AT SINGAPORE THEY BOARDED another boat, the *William Bullock,* on April 9, 1938, and steamed into the harbor at Kuching, Sarawak, two days later. Joshua and Eunice strained to gather in all the sights of this new land. A row of waving coconut palms and mangrove shrubs greeted their eyes. On the wharf both Malay and Chinese coolies scurried around, loading and unloading cargo from boats berthed along the shore. Everywhere the little sampans (dinghies) bobbed up and down on the murky water.

"Is anybody here to meet us?" Joshua muttered, his heart pounding apprehensively.

She scanned the faces on the shore. "And how will they ever be able to pick us out among the crowd on the dock?"

Her husband felt through his wallet for a couple photos given him by the union secretary. Glancing anxiously back and forth from photos to crowd, they searched for any familiar face.

"There—that's them!" Joshua exclaimed joyously.

Sure enough, there were the beaming faces of Pastor John M. Nerness, the director and treasurer of the Sarawak Mission, and Mr. Chu Sing Fatt, principal of Sunny Hill School. Legs trembling with relief, Joshua and Eunice watched as the two men bounded up the gangplank with outstretched hands. "Welcome to Sarawak!" they said again and again. "We are so glad to see you!"

Depositing the wide-eyed young couple and their luggage in the rear seat of an old Model-T Ford, pastor and principal acted as animated tour guides as the car chugged along.

But there's nothing here, Eunice thought in despair, her heart sinking. *This isn't anything like Guangzhou or Hong Kong.*

True enough, at first glance it appeared to her that the town of Kuching consisted of only one street lined by stores on both sides. The road leading to the school campus was rocky and in some places unpaved. And as the campus came into view, Eunice's heart plummeted even further.

"I can't believe it," she murmured in Joshua's ear, her voice masked by the noisy engine. "These buildings have *thatched roofs.*"

Pastor Nerness steered the little car to a stop in front of a small thatched hut with a porch. Standing in front were a young Chinese woman with a little girl.

"This is your house," Mr. Chu announced. "And that's my wife and little girl. We're your neighbors."

Eunice brightened slightly. *Well,* she thought, *at least I'll have a young Chinese woman next door.*

After depositing their luggage in the house, the two men took Joshua and Eunice on a tour of the school campus.

The Chongs' first home was this thatched-roof stilt house in Kuching, in the state of Sarawak. Eunice holds Baby Mary.

59

Sunny Hill School, they learned, had been established as a result of the vision of a dedicated church member who had emigrated from Guangzhou to live with his two daughters and sons-in-law. One son-in-law was a dentist and the other a businessman, and they had set up both clinic and store in the same building. As they actively witnessed in their business places, a group of believers began meeting there, and soon the building was too small to accommodate them.

At the suggestion of their father-in-law, the two young men bought an almost five-acre lot on Rock Road to build not only a church but also a school for its members' children. By the time Joshua and Eunice arrived, the enrollment had reached 61 students, with a faculty of five teachers of Chinese and Indonesian origin.

"Eunice," Joshua asked some months later. "Is something the matter?"

"I'm homesick," she told him frankly.

Puzzled, he stared at her. "Homesick? I haven't even thought much about home since we got here."

"Well, that's no surprise. You're the pastor, always out visiting and getting acquainted with people or working on the classes you're teaching at school. I haven't had much to do except unpack."

He sighed sympathetically. "You're not looking too well."

"I'm *not* well," she said. "I think"—and she watched his face carefully—"that I have morning sickness."

Her young husband glanced at her with concern. "Morning sickness? What's that?" And when she told him, he took her in his arms, and the two of them pondered the adventurous life they'd accepted and what the future might hold for the tiny baby growing within her.

Having an understanding mate didn't make life any easier for the young mother-to-be. Accustomed to a temperate climate, Eunice found the tropics insufferable. Back home she'd relished the snows of winter, the freshness of spring, the colors of autumn, and the moderate warmth of summer.

"Doesn't Sarawak have four seasons?" she asked her neighbor, Mrs. Chu.

The other woman nodded. "Of course," she chuckled, naming them on her fingers. "Warm, warmer, hotter, and hottest!"

Eunice eyed her gloomily. "That is not very comforting. My face is always so sweaty. And it seems as if the only way to get relief from the heat is to take showers."

"It took me a while to get used to it too," Mrs. Chu said understandingly.

The only real excitement the weather provided was during the monsoon season. Then the rain poured down in torrents, the lightning flashed, and the thunder crashed. Eunice had never seen a thunderstorm up close. Back in her part of China, thunder was only a distant rumble and the rain usually a light sprinkle. The first time a thunderstorm crashed overhead, Joshua found her cowering under the sheets, shaking with terror, eyes squeezed shut so that she wouldn't see the dazzling flashes.

And the flowers are different here, she thought mournfully. *I miss the tulips, the daffodils, and those azaleas that dotted the campus of my nursing school.* Here she saw only the red "flame of the forest," the bougainvillea, and the yellow frangipani.

The fruits were different too. The markets had scarcely any of the ones she'd enjoyed at home—peaches, cherries, longans, lychees, persimmons, and pears. Here she could find only mangoes, papayas, pineapples, and a spiky fruit she'd never seen before.

"What's that?" she asked when she saw Mrs. Chu eating one.

"Durian," her neighbor told her, digging out the rich, creamy pulp from the fruit's center. "It's yummy. Try some."

"It has a really strange odor, doesn't it?"

"But it *tastes* good. Come on, give it a try."

"Not right now, thanks," Eunice said politely, trying to conceal a shudder. *I'm going to put a mile between myself and that obnoxious, stinky durian,* she decided.

By this time Eunice had made quite a number of friends, and they finally decided to gang up on her. "Try some durian, Eunice," they begged her. "Otherwise you'll never know what you're missing." Day after day they pestered her.

"All right," she finally sighed. "I'll try it, just to get you off my back."

Screwing up her face and pinching her nose, she popped a durian seed into her mouth. As it touched her palate, her eyes opened wide in surprise. It was the best fruit she'd ever tasted! As sweet as honey and as soft as ice cream, it melted in her mouth.

Watching her expression, her friends laughed with delight. "What do you think, Eunice? It's not too bad, is it?"

Without answering she reached for another helping, then another, and still another.

Now her friends were laughing helplessly. "Watch out," somebody said. "Your stomach's going to burst."

"She's an addict!" another woman giggled.

Ever afterward, whenever the fruit was in season, her friends saw her perched on a stool with a newspaper spread on the floor, the pungent fruit piled high on it, as she devoured durian after durian.

Another thing that puzzled Eunice at first was why the local people wanted to torture themselves by heaping hot chili pepper on their food and eating curried meat and vegetables that burned all the way down their throats. She could not foresee the day when curry would become her favorite dish and chili pepper a part of her diet.

However, with the new year she had other things to think about besides weather and food. Toward the end of the year she and Joshua received a belated Christmas gift in the arrival of their first child, a daughter. They named her Mary Hui-Tze—Mary because she was born just after Christmas, and Hui-Tze (wisdom and tenderness) in the hope that she would acquire such qualities as she grew up.

Eunice was soon learning on the job how to be a new mother. At the same time, having gotten her nursing license from the Kuching Health Department, she also kept busy delivering other women's babies. Her services were soon in great demand from the campus wives as well as the townspeople.

For his part, Joshua continued to work with his colleagues to expand the church and school. Every Friday evening and Saturday afternoon they visited the homes of the students to meet their parents and people in the neighborhood. They spent the school vacation conducting evangelistic meetings.

And they didn't forget the school's future, either. Before classes resumed in the fall, the teachers traveled to the surrounding villages to visit each home and to recruit students. The personal persuasion paid off—the fall term began with more than 100 students, almost double the previous year's enrollment. When the school employed more Chinese and English teachers, enrollment bulged again. Faculty and students then went out to solicit funds from the public to build new buildings and to get grants from the government to subsidize the construction projects.

Everything was looking bright for the school when tragedy struck.

One day Joshua's Chinese language students were taking a test when a huge explosion rocked the classroom walls. Startled, he glanced out the window just in time to see a human torch flashing by. He raced out of the classroom, with his class following closely behind. On the field next to the school building was a young boy on fire from head to toe, rolling from side to side on the ground.

As a huge crowd of teachers and students watched in horror, wringing their hands and screaming hysterically, one of the teachers dashed up with a bucket of water and poured it over the writhing figure. The flame was extinguished, and the stench of burning flesh filled the air. The ambulance arrived soon after, and its attendants put the horribly burned boy on a stretcher and took him away to the nearest hospital. With third-degree burns over 90 percent of his body, he died soon afterward.

The administration immediately began investigating what had caused the tragic accident. According to the boy's classmates, the intelligent and adventuresome child had been intrigued by the drums of gasoline stored in one of the work sheds on the school grounds. Evidently he had stolen into the shed and lit a match to look at the gasoline. A spark from the match ignited it and triggered the huge explosion that enveloped him in flames.

For days afterward the spectacle of the flaming child writhing on the ground haunted the staff and students. Many a night Mr. Chin, the teacher who'd extinguished the flame and a neighbor of Joshua's, would pound on the wall, crying out in terror, because the image of the dead boy hounded him in his nightmares. Guilt overwhelmed him when he learned that the water he had thrown on the boy had in part contributed to his death.

"What I needed to extinguish the fire were blankets, not water," he kept sobbing and moaning. "But in my panic I didn't think of that."

The sobering experience deeply affected the faculty and students, clouding the atmosphere in the school for a long time. To prevent any more of such tragedies, the administration took additional measures to improve the security of the school and to provide a safer environment for the increasing number of students.

But, though mercifully hidden from them at the moment, a far worse threat would hit them at the turn of the new school year.

10

Invaded by Air and Sea

SOUND ASLEEP BESIDE EUNICE, Joshua jerked violently awake on the morning of December 8, 1941. For an instant the explosion mingled with his dream. But he didn't have time to sort out reality from nightmare.

Boom! BOOM!

Eunice was awake now, clutching him tightly with sleep-sweaty fingers. "Joshua! What—?"

Wriggling out of her grasp, he tumbled off the bed and found his way to the window by the faint light of dawn. He had scarcely reached it when another boom rattled the walls. "Let's get out of here!" he shouted.

His wife gasped. "We can't go *outside!*"

"It's safer than in here," he told her. "Go grab Mary. I'll see what's going on."

Swinging the front door open, he paused in the doorway. In the distance a huge cloud of smoke billowed skyward. "Bombs!" he shouted back over his shoulder, and then the terrifying wail of the air-raid siren filled the early-morning air.

A loud unfamiliar voice suddenly blared through the room. Eunice had turned on the radio. "Those can't be Japanese bombs already," she shouted above it, adjusting the volume with one hand while cradling 2-year-old Mary with the other. "They bombed Pearl Harbor only yesterday. What would they want with Borneo?"

"They want *everything,*" Joshua said grimly. "Quiet. Here comes the newscast."

Together they listened as a breathless announcer told the terrifying tidings. Sure enough, the invasion of Sarawak by the Japanese air force had begun. Sometime back the country had allied itself with Germany and Italy, and since the Pearl Harbor attack would no doubt draw the United States into the conflict, Japan was wasting no time in grasping all the territory it could.

And from that day on, Borneo found itself fully embroiled in the war. Mail between Borneo and China instantly ceased and would not resume for four years. Joshua and Eunice lost all contact with friends and relatives at home.

And things had been going so well. Two years after arriving in Kuching, Joshua, together with his colleagues in Sunny Hill School, had witnessed the phenomenal growth of the school from 62 to more than 200 students. They had erected new buildings and employed additional teachers to serve the new pupils. The staff had felt a real sense of achievement and had been looking forward to the Christmas festivities.

Joshua and Eunice had sensed the distant rumble of the Second World War raging on the European front, and they knew that China was firmly in the grip of the Japanese. But even when they learned about the bombing of Pearl Harbor on December 7, they had felt little concern. Borneo had been relatively sheltered from the war brewing in other parts of the world. What happened this morning, therefore, was a rude and bitter awakening for everyone.

"Let's just hope," Joshua said glumly, "that the Japanese soldiers find themselves so busy everywhere else that they don't plant their boots on Sarawak."

In the days that followed, order after order came from the Sarawak city authorities, relayed by radio broadcasts.

"We are organizing first-aid groups to attend to the casualties. . . . Because towns will be bombing targets, all stores will be closed until further notice, and all townspeople must evacuate immediately . . ."

Less publicly, the authorities quickly rounded up all of Borneo's Japanese residents and herded them into concentration camps to keep them from collaborating with any invasion forces that might show up. Ground and naval forces—augmented by newly arriving British and Indonesian forces—mobilized and stationed themselves at strategic positions. Some of the soldiers received orders to link with local police to protect the evacuated homes and stores from looters.

Though the government tried hard to maintain calm, each air-raid siren shattered nerves. Understanding that war meant food shortages, citizens scrambled madly to stash away as much as possible. Then they prepared to endure the hardship ahead.

But on Christmas Eve they dropped their guard.

"Let's push aside our worries for one night and just celebrate," they told each other. "After all, why would the Japanese want to launch an attack on a day that commemorates peace and joy? Surely they have that much decency. Anyway, our coasts are heavily guarded."

So the Christmas parties began. Even the town's militias relaxed. Two of the British soldiers stationed by a river close to the coast happened to glance out a barracks window. "Look at those trees in the distance," one said. "They're waving."

"Great!" said the other. "Good news."

"Why good news?"

"A storm's brewing. No invasion on Christmas Eve."

But Christmas morning dawned stormless—bright and clear. The soldiers awoke, feeling great after a fun-filled and restful night. "Silent night, holy night," one warbled at the top of his voice as he again glanced out of the barracks windows.

Then he blinked in disbelief. "What's that?" he yelped.

"What are you looking at?" someone asked, drifting over to join him.

"Out there! Are my eyes playing tricks? Or are those—"

"Japs!" howled the other. "They're swarming all over the place! Let's get out of here!" Yanking on his trousers, he bolted for the door.

Pandemonium broke out in the barracks. Soldiers leaped out of bed, lunged outside, and jumped into their jeeps, many leaving their weapons behind. The terrified convoy roared into town, the soldiers screaming, "The Japs are here! The Japs are here! They're right behind us!"

Indeed, in the silence of the night, dark shadowy figures donning snorkels had plunged into the Sarawak River. The Japanese marines, under the cover of darkness and camouflaged by tree branches—whose waving indicated a far different kind of storm—had swum up the river at high tide and landed on its banks on Christmas Day. The flight of the defending soldiers left everything wide open for the invaders to march into town without any resistance, and Japan added Sarawak to its list of conquests.

Once in town, the Japanese military took immediate steps to strengthen their hold. Swiftly occupying all the government buildings, they arrested the important officials before they could organize any resistance. Grudgingly the authorities announced that the people should stay calm and cooperate with their captors. The invaders also took the British and Indonesian soldiers as prisoners of war. When they released all the Japanese residents confined in the concentration camps, many of the internees began helping the new rulers track down anyone involved in the resistance movement. Soon the enemy had firm control of the country.

"This is worse than I thought it would be," Joshua growled to Eunice one day after returning from an errand.

"You mean the roadblocks?"

"That's bad enough. They're screening everybody, no exceptions. But when you get to the checkpoint, they make you stop and bow to the guards."

"I'd never do that!" she snapped.

"If you don't, they slap you around. Or kick you. Or just make you stand at attention under the hot sun."

His wife shuddered. "So that's why not a lot of people from out here are going into town."

"Might as well not bother if they don't have to," he agreed. "But nobody's stopping the looters. They've been breaking into the stores at night and carrying off everything."

"Are the Japanese soldiers *beasts?*" Eunice said scornfully. "Don't they realize that if everything's looted, they won't have any supplies left for themselves?"

"I guess they're too busy consolidating their power."

Finally, with the arrival of reinforcements, the occupation forces turned their attention to the looters and took drastic measures to stop them.

"All looters who are arrested will be beheaded," they announced, "and their heads will be hung up in public places as a warning to other fools. And all stolen goods must be returned. Anyone who disobeys will be tortured as well as beheaded."

However, the real threat for Joshua and other church leaders was the secret police, as well as traitorous citizens who'd become informants. The Japanese military, acting on intelligence they received (real or trumped-up), started arresting school administrators and other prominent leaders of organizations, especially foreigners from America or Britain. The soldiers hauled them away for interrogation, sometimes torturing them to find out if they had participated in any anti-Japanese activities. When found guilty, they were imprisoned and tortured even more severely. Fear gripped everyone's hearts—who would be next? Often those taken away were never seen or heard of again, having perished through torture or execution.

I'm principal of Sunny Hill School, Joshua reminded himself. *I wonder when they'll come for me.*

Since the new Japanese government had confiscated Sunny Hill School and the church to serve as barracks for the soldiers, the mission and school administration had decided to move their personnel to another mission school campus at Ayer Manis in the suburbs of Kuching.

One day Joshua and Mr. Chin, another member of the school staff, were busy in his office packing documents for the transfer when the door crashed open. A dreaded Japanese secret police officer strode in.

"*Chong-san* [Mr. Chong]?" he inquired.

Joshua swallowed. "Y-yes?"

"*Isshoni keisatsusho ni kinasai* [Come with us to the police station]!" he barked.

The blood drained from Joshua's face. *Is there a way to escape?* His eyes flicked to the window, then to two burly soldiers blocking the door. *No time!* he thought desperately. *No time to say goodbye to Eunice and Mary.*

Quickly he turned to the terrified Mr. Chin. "Please," he whispered. "Tell my wife what has happened to me. And if I don't come back—please take care of her and Mary for me."

His friend nodded and watched in helpless terror as the soldiers tumbled Joshua into the back of a truck and drove him away. As soon as they were out of sight, Mr. Chin raced to the Chong home, burst through the door, and gasped out his terrible story.

Standing there staring at him, Eunice was too terrified even to thank him. She said only two syllables—a feeble "Mary"—then gathered her child into her arms and sank to the floor, sobbing loudly.

Mr. Chin tiptoed out of the room. Already the distraught young mother's wailing had brought friends and neighbors running from adjacent houses. "What can we do? How can we help?" they asked her.

"Pray" was all she could whisper. "For Joshua. For his safety."

11

Enemy Occupation

THE HOURS DRAGGED ALONG. Night came, and a couple of Eunice's friends volunteered to stay with her. She sobbed out her gratitude, but soon they were asleep, and she spent a sleepless night anticipating her fate as a young widow. The next day crawled by, but still no sign of Joshua, and Eunice found herself swinging between hope and despair.

The third day she slept late, with Mary beside her. Even after she'd awakened, she lay still, deep in a pit of depression.

What is there to get out of bed for? she asked herself. *The love of my life, the provider for my child, is dead.*

Suddenly she heard a soft knock on the door.

One of the women, Eunice thought. As she arose and walked to the door, she braced herself to be cheerful. But a smile would not come, no matter how she tried. Slowly she opened the door.

Joshua stood there in front of her!

His hair was disheveled, but his eyes were bright with tears of joy. He literally bounced into the room.

"Ohhhh, my darlings," he said again and again, wrapping Eunice and Mary in his arms. "Praise God! Praise God, I'm home again!"

Eunice would not let go of him, but held his face between her hands and stared and stared at him. "Wha—what happened?" she finally babbled. "What—why—how did you—"

"God has been very good to me," he said with a deep trembling sigh.

"Did they—did they hurt you?"

He shook his head. "They asked me a lot of questions."

"What about? You've done nothing wrong!"

"About the mission school," he said. "The Japanese are deeply suspicious of anything connected with the Americans, especially Christians. But they didn't torture me."

"Thank heaven."

"Remember," he said firmly. "Mary, are you listening too? This was not luck. It is the providence of God that has saved me from torture or even death!"

As the Japanese occupation of Sarawak dragged on, local residents—especially the mission and Sunny Hill School staff now located at Ayer Manis—faced increasing deprivations.

"Joshua, it won't be long before we'll starve," Eunice told her husband one day. "Now our rations are down to four katis [about five and a half pounds] of rice per person per month. I'm going to have to start boiling it with yams and tapioca. The Chins say they have heard that the rations are going to be cut even more. Why can't the authorities find more food for us?"

He sighed. "All trade with the outside world is cut off. But at least the Japanese are starting to think about our needs. They're ordering us to go out to the less-dense jungles and plant things."

"Such as?"

"Yams, peanuts, corn, rice, vegetables, tapioca."

"But we need food *now.*"

Sure enough, the rations shrank still further. Joshua and his colleagues were forced into the backbreaking job of chopping down forest trees to clear the land for agriculture. It was then that he recognized how God had prepared him for this difficult experience. Back in China, while attending college, he'd taken a year of industrial arts training. He had spent a year working on the college farm, which meant that he was now able to wrest food from the land while supplementing the family's meager diet with wild ferns, mushrooms, and fruits found in the jungle.

The school and mission personnel lived together as one big family, and the circumstances they shared in common drew them closer to each other and to God. Every day the mission director and treasurer, Pastor William W. R. Lake, conducted their devotional period, and they had prayer bands three times a day.

Meanwhile, Joshua made frequent trips from Ayer Manis to downtown Kuching to minister to the church members by holding meetings in their homes and taking them some food supplies. He also wanted to keep an eye on the property now occupied by the Japanese soldiers.

However, pedaling his bicycle 37 miles each way soon exhausted him and proved to be too hazardous. Since his family was safe with others on the campus of Ayer Manis, he decided to remain in Kuching, visiting his family whenever he could. Later, when the new government restored part of the church and school property to the mission, he was able move his family back into town. Together with three single teachers who accompanied him, they lived on the campus of Sunny Hill School.

Any hope of liberation for the people in Sarawak faded as other countries in Southeast Asia fell. The Japanese continued to advance relentlessly toward the Philippines and Indonesia, and everyone knew that their ambitious plans included all of eastern Asia and even Australia.

Often Joshua apologized for not being able to spend more time with his family.

"Don't worry," his wife said. "I'm busy too."

"What are you doing?"

"Delivering babies. Once word gets out that I'm a nurse, every woman who can't afford a hospital stay wants me to be her midwife. Babies won't wait until the war is over."

The worry lines in his face deepened. "Don't work too hard."

"I'm strong," she insisted. "And they pay me."

"With what? Nobody has any money."

"Vegetables. Chickens, too. I've got a brood of 10 already, and they're keeping us supplied with eggs."

His eyebrows shot up. "I *thought* I heard some clucking in the backyard."

Though she didn't tell her husband right away, Eunice had another reason for being happy with the extra eggs. Even her closest friends didn't know that she was engaged in a secret project that might have cost her her head if the authorities had found out about it.

The idea for it came to her one day as she and little Mary were walking home from the nearby store.

"Mama, look." The child pointed. "Why do all those men have chains on their legs?"

72

Eunice's grip on her hand tightened convulsively. "They're prisoners of war. And look how thin they are. They're hungry."

The POWs, scarcely more than skin and bones, were staggering down the road from the bombed-out airport where they had been doing reconstruction work under the burning sun all day. Their eyes, staring out of gaunt sockets, were filled with pain and despair. One of the men suddenly thudded to the ground.

"Mama, that man fell down."

Quickly Eunice put her hand over her daughter's eyes. "He's hot and tired, and he has fainted."

But Mary peeked out from around her mother's hand and saw two guards run toward the man and start slapping him to revive him. The child screeched in alarm. Even though she was only 2 years old, she felt pity toward such victims of the war. She would see many examples of such inhuman treatment during the weary years ahead. The half-starved POWs would often resort to eating the roots and barks of trees and even the snails crawling in the bushes. Many died of food poisoning as a result.

For days afterward the scene haunted her mother, too. *What can I do for these pathetic men?* Eunice asked herself. *There's no way I can stop the harsh treatment they're getting, of course. But maybe there's some way I can ease some of their hunger without putting myself and my family at risk.*

Eunice thought long and hard about the situation, because the authorities would consider anyone caught helping the captives as engaging in anti-Japanese activities and might severely punish or even execute them.

The next time the POWs passed by, Eunice was ready. Leaving Mary in the care of friends, she stationed herself next to the hedge separating the school compound from the road. Hidden within her loose blouse were a few balls of rice and some boiled eggs. When the guards weren't looking her way, she swiftly passed the food to the POW closest to her, and just as swiftly he hid the food.

I've got to come up with another plan, she told herself that night. *It's too risky to hand them the food myself. I'll hide it in the bushes and try to signal where it is.*

In the days that followed she participated in an ingenious game of cat-and-mouse. When the POWs saw Eunice standing by the hedge, their eyes would brighten, and they would create a distraction. While the guards dealt with the commotion, someone would snatch the little package from under a clump of weeds.

Since her little brood of hens provided a portion of the lifesaving food, it really disturbed her to find something amiss in her chicken coop one morning.

Strange, she thought as she bent down to feed the chickens. *Are they all here? I'm sure I had 10.* She counted them twice to make sure. *Nine. What happened?*

A few days later another chicken had disappeared. *Some kind of wild animal,* she decided. *I'll chain our dog outside the coop to watch it.* That worked for a while, but one day, to her horror and grief, she found her faithful guard stretched out dead outside the chicken coop—poisoned.

So the chicken thief is human, she thought grimly. *I'll catch him red-handed.* Besides stringing tiny bells to the door and the walls of the chicken coop, she also carefully marked the remaining chickens. Every tinkle of the bell sent her flying to the window, and for a while no more chickens vanished.

But one day she spotted the thief. *My eyes must be deceiving me,* she thought. Flabbergasted, she watched as her neighbor (who was neither a church member nor a school employee) darted away from the coop, a squawking hen gripped tightly in his hand.

Eyes aflame with fury, Eunice strode into his yard, ready to do battle with the chicken thief. Unfortunately, she was too late! He had already started slaughtering the chicken. Because he had plucked all the feathers, she could not prove that it was hers. Helpless, she turned to leave. However, she couldn't resist delivering a parting shot.

"How very nice," she said sweetly, burning holes in him with her eyes. "You're so *lucky* to have chicken for dinner. Someone has been helping himself to *my* chickens and robbing my family and me of much-needed food."

Smiling blandly, the man said nothing.

"I think I know who the thief is," she continued in a voice of chilled steel, "and if I catch him at it again, I will immediately report him to the police."

The man's gaze shifted, and his smile got a little lopsided. Eunice could tell that he was remembering exactly the same thing she was: the Japanese occupiers severely punished all criminals, including thieves. Leaving him to think things over, she turned on her heel and walked away.

The threat worked, and she was able to continue her POW relief efforts until the end of the war.

However, in the uncertain atmosphere neither Eunice nor Joshua could ever feel entirely safe. One day as Mary played in the front yard Eunice went into the house to get something and happened to glance out the window to see if her daughter was still safe.

Stunned, she caught sight of a pair of Japanese officers gripping the child tightly by her hands. She raced outside, but froze as the two men approached the house.

"Konnichwa," one of the officers said. *"Ojyosan wo Eiga ni otsure shitain-odesuga."* (Good afternoon. We would like to take your daughter with us to the movies.)

Eunice was speechless. Except for the greeting, she couldn't understand a word he was saying. Her husband could understand Japanese, but though he was home, he was nowhere in sight at the moment.

Mary started to whimper.

Receiving no response, the two men turned away, Mary still between them. In spite of the girl's confused wails, they lifted her into a small jeep-like military vehicle and chugged away down the street.

12

When Death Rained Out of the Sky

J OSHUA!" SHE SCREAMED as she burst into the house, sobbing hysterically. "They've taken her away!"

Her husband's puzzled face peered around a doorway.

"Did you hear what I said? *They've kidnapped her!*"

He blinked. "Kidnapped whom?"

"The Japanese soldiers took Mary!"

His heart almost stopped beating. "They don't kidnap *children*" was all he could think to say. "Adults, yes. Children, no."

Eunice pushed him to the door. "She's *gone!* She's *gone!*"

Coming to his senses, he dashed outside. In the distance he could still see the military vehicle, his little daughter waving back at him. Helpless and hopeless, the parents could only drop to their knees. "Dear heavenly Father," they prayed, hardly able to summon the strength to speak, "please protect her. Father, she is our only child. Our only child."

Hearing Eunice's screams, neighbors began to gather. They surrounded the kneeling, weeping couple and tried to reassure them.

Two hours later the little car bounced back up the street again and squeaked to a stop in front of their house. The grieving parents dashed out of the house to see the Japanese officers emerging from the vehicle. Mary jumped down and ran toward her parents, smiling happily and jabbering about a movie she had seen.

Before Joshua could even speak, one of the officers apologized.

"My name is Yamada," he said, grinning sheepishly. "Sorry about what happened. But we just couldn't help it. We haven't seen our own kids for months and months. So when we saw your sweet little daughter, we decided to borrow her for a couple hours and give her a treat."

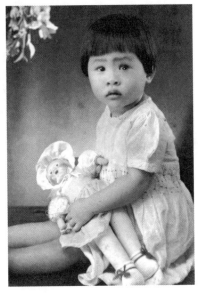

On Christmas Day 1941 the Japanese invaded Sarawak, Borneo. One day during the subsequent occupation, two soldiers, homesick for their families in Japan, were driving by the Chong house. Spotting little Mary in the front yard, they couldn't resist temporarily "kidnapping" her and taking her to see a movie!

Though Eunice was still scowling, relief washed over Joshua. *Thank You, heavenly Father,* he prayed silently.

From that day onward Mr. Yamada—a pilot in the Japanese air force—was a regular visitor in their home. Sometimes he brought his buddies with him. "You don't know how nice it feels," they said gratefully, "just to sit in a living room in a real house. And to get a chance to hold a child and hear her voice."

In time Joshua became good friends with Mr. Yamada and some of the other officers. *Friends among my foes,* he thought to himself. *How ironic. But now I see that suffering happens not only to the captives but also to the captors. These men are real people, trapped between having to execute their country's expansionist policies and their own better judgment.*

His new friends confessed that the atrocities some of their comrades had inflicted greatly pained them. "We've devastated your country—we know that," they said. "But when an army invades another country, everybody's on edge. It's kill or be killed. Our instinct for survival has led us to do things that still haunt us."

77

Joshua began to realize that the Japanese soldiers were also beings capable of feelings of warmth and love, and who furthermore suffered the pain of separation from loved ones and family. With this new insight, Joshua was able to thank God that he was the one being persecuted and not the one doing it. The experience also gave him solid reasons to love everyone—including his enemies.

One day Mr. Yamada stood at Joshua's doorstep to say farewell. "Good news," he said. "I'm flying back to Japan for a short visit to my family. Thank you very much for your kindness and your friendship." He smiled his sheepish grin again. "And thank you for loaning me Mary!"

Not too long afterward Joshua learned to his sorrow that Mr. Yamada had died when Allied forces shot his plane down over the South China Sea.

By 1944 the British decided that it was time to reclaim their lost colonies. The Japanese forces, spread thin over the wide territory of their conquest and repulsed with heavy losses to their navy after an attack on Australia, had been considerably weakened. After heavy fighting between them and Allied soldiers in the South Pacific islands, the Japanese soldiers had begun to retreat.

Not long after this Allied B-19s began bombing and strafing the Japanese military emplacements in Sarawak. Such missions rapidly became more frequent, with air-raid sirens constantly piercing the air. "Your day of liberation is near!" proclaimed leaflets that rained out of the sky.

While jubilant that the air-raids heralded the day of their freedom, the residents of Kuching were fearful that they would experience the irony of losing their lives just as the war ended. Their fear became very real when the occupation army, desperate to increase its air defenses, rounded up the civilians and, despite the rumbling bombers overhead, set them to work alongside British POWs to repair bombed-out airports and even build new ones.

The Japanese posted secret police in such areas to prevent the civilians from joining forces with the POWs to stage an uprising, forcing the people to appear to cooperate with the Japanese while praying hard that they would not get killed by friendly fire. The Japanese soldiers, on the other hand, knowing that their days were numbered, began planning their own escape.

It was at this time that Joshua, who'd become a fluent speaker of

78

Japanese, found himself conscripted to work at the airport as a translator. On one such day he and a group of people were laboring in a small airport when the air-raid siren shattered the air.

"*Mizo wo hotte, de* . . . [Dig a trench and . . .]," he translated, then stopped in midsentence. "Help!" he cried. "There's no air-raid shelter here!"

The Japanese supervisors and the POWs were fleeing in every different direction, but Joshua stood rooted to the ground in terror. *Vroom! Boom! Crash!* He could hear bombs already exploding at another airport in the distance. Silver wings glinting in the sunlight, one of the Allied bombers banked low and approached.

Run, you fool! Joshua thought to himself. Eyes bulging in fright, he dived into the part of the trench that they had already dug. But as the plane roared closer he realized how vulnerable his position was. Scrambling out of the trench, he raced across the landing strip and into the bushes at the edge of the rubber plantation next to the airfield. He burrowed his head into the underbrush, closed his eyes, and kept desperately and aimlessly pushing himself deeper into the undergrowth.

Vroom! Boom! Crash! Vroom! Boom! Crash! The earth shook with thunderous explosions. Joshua paused, opened his eyes a bit, and turned to see more bombs raining down from the sky, some landing only about 400 feet from where he was, hurling debris skyward and turning rubber trees into torches. Then other bombers approached in wave after wave, dropping their deadly cargo.

Digging his face into the soft ground, he could taste the soil in his mouth, but he didn't care. He wished the earth would open up and shield him from the death raining out of the sky. As the explosions continued, he burrowed still further through the bushes.

"God, help me!" he cried aloud, and began to recite, " 'Even though I walk through the valley of the shadow of death, I will fear no evil, for you are with me.' 'God is our refuge and strength, an ever-present help in trouble. Therefore we will not fear, though the earth give way and the mountains fall into the heart of the sea, though its waters roar and foam and the mountains quake with their surging.' Lord," he shouted, "I claim these promises! Please save me!"

Then all of a sudden everything went silent, and the drone of aircraft faded in the distance. After waiting for what seemed an eternity, Joshua lifted his head slowly and peered out. When he was sure that no more bombers were heading his way, he crawled cautiously out from under the undergrowth.

The scene that met his eyes sent him reeling. Charred bodies and grotesque headless corpses lay everywhere. Bits and pieces of flesh plastered the trunks of the trees. The airport by which he had been standing only moments before had disappeared, and in its place were huge craters around which the charred bodies or remnants of bodies were draped.

Head swimming and stomach wrenching, Joshua covered his mouth and turned away. As if in afterthought, he checked himself. His pants were torn and tattered, his knees bruised, and his face scratched and bleeding—but he was alive.

Then a new terror twisted his heart. *Where were Eunice and Mary? Our house is located too close to this airport. Have they been killed?*

Stumbling out of the heavily cratered airfield, he tried to find his way home, but was confused for a moment, because the road leading home had disappeared. By its side lay huge trees, their roots pointing skyward, and piles of rubble covered everything. Then he got his bearings and plunged into a field, eventually reaching downtown Kuching.

There an even greater scene of devastation met his eyes. Screaming people stood where houses had once lined the streets, frantically clawing through more rubble with their bare hands, trying to retrieve their possessions or to rescue loved ones. Others stood dazed and in shock, unable to move. Ambulance sirens filled the air.

Oh, heavenly Father . . . oh, heavenly Father . . .

As he neared his home, his heart threatened to stop beating. A house next to his had been leveled, and a huge crater had replaced a nearby field. A crowd stood in front of Joshua's house, and he numbly noticed that explosions had blasted its windows clean of glass, its front door was a gaping hole, and the house itself sagged precariously. As he rounded one corner he saw why—one entire wall had vanished.

Fear surged through his weary muscles. "Eunice! Mary!" he screamed.

"Don't go in, Joshua!" someone shouted. "It's not safe! Wait for—"

Shoving the man aside, Joshua dove through the doorway hole.

13

Liberation!

AT FIRST EVERYTHING WAS eerily silent except for the creaking timbers overhead. Then from a corner he heard a small whimper and discovered his wife and daughter cowering under a desk, their eyes wide with terror. At the sight of Joshua they stumbled toward him and flew into his arms. Ignoring the dangerously shifting structure above him, he knelt and pulled them down beside him, and once again sent praises and thanksgiving heavenward.

Later Eunice told him what had happened.

"Early this morning," she said, "I'd asked Stella if she could come with me to look at that rental house we're trying to decide on. She brought her little daughter Netty with her. We were looking the house over when we heard the air-raid sirens."

"Why didn't you run to the air-raid shelter?"

"We just froze from fright. Also, the two girls would have slowed us down. So rather than risk getting caught in the open, we ran into this tiny lean-to next to the house—just in time. The bombs had already started dropping in the distance.

"We watched it all through the little opening in the lean-to. We saw the bombs whistle down to earth, and then there'd be this thunderous crash, and the lean-to walls would tremble. Every once in a while the whole structure would sway, threatening to topple over and bury us alive."

Joshua lifted grateful eyes heavenward once more. Then he took a deep breath for a firm husbandly lecture. "Next time, Eunice—" he began.

"I know, I know. Get to the shelter at all costs. Anyway, our kids were clinging so tightly to us that I thought we'd suffocate, and all four of us were crying. Finally I just began to repeat Bible verses out loud. I did as much as I could remember of Psalm 91."

Her husband shuddered. "I was reciting similar verses out at the airport."

"Then I just got down on my knees," she continued, "and pleaded for God to protect us. Suddenly I realized that the children had stopped crying, and everything seemed quiet outside. The last wave of bombers had come and gone.

"We waited for a while. Then we slowly crept out of the shelter. It was horrible. Lots of buildings had been flattened and burned, and there were dead people lying everywhere. We covered the girls' eyes and just kept running as fast as we could. Finally I got home and saw the damage."

He shuddered again. "But you still went inside?"

"I didn't know if the bombers would come back. Mary and I just huddled under that desk and wondered if we would ever see you again."

On August 6 and 9, 1945, the American air force dropped atomic bombs on Hiroshima and Nagasaki. Japan surrendered less than a week later, ending three years and eight months of enemy occupation in Sarawak. As Allied soldiers made a triumphant landing in Kuching, the Japanese soldiers surrendered. The liberators took them to the concentration camps and released the POWs and foreigners interned in the camps.

The former captives subjected their former captors to the same hard labor and other harsh treatment the Japanese had inflicted. Soon starving, the Japanese soldiers found themselves forced to eat snails, and many became little more than skin and bones. Fortunately for them, however, an exchange of POWs took place not too long after the conclusion of war, and they went home to Japan.

For the majority of the residents in Sarawak the end of war brought the liberty they once enjoyed, and they were able to pick up their lives where they left off. But for some, liberation did not turn out to be the blessing it was supposed to be.

"Did you ever meet Mr. Lee?" Joshua asked Eunice one day.

"Once, I think," she replied. "Isn't he the one that's gotten so rich? The Japanese occupation made him a lot of money."

"That's the man. I just talked to someone who saw him yesterday. Mr.

Lee was a millionaire last week and a pauper today. And now all he does is sit in his house with his sacks of worthless money, counting the bills again and again, crying and laughing at the same time. He's gone completely crazy."

"Serves him right," Eunice said unsympathetically.

Those who had had the foresight and faith to plan on a day of deliverance found resuming the life of prewar days less traumatic. As the war had begun, Eunice had carefully sealed her money and other possessions in cans and buried them in the yard behind her house. Now she was able to retrieve them and help the family's financial condition. The Chong family had come through the war relatively unscathed.

One day she heard several voices outside her door and a firm, steady knocking.

Who's this? she wondered, a tingle of worry in her chest. *The occupation's over. It can't be the secret police.* Cautiously she opened the door a crack and peered out.

In the sunshine stood several lean men with smiles on their faces.

Eunice flung wide the door. "I know who you are!" she gasped. "Come in, come in!"

Through the door crowded some of the POWs she'd secretly fed during the war years. "We didn't even learn your name," said one who spoke her language, "until we started asking around your neighborhood. But we have come to personally express our gratitude to you for all you did for us, and for putting your life in danger."

And then they began reaching into their pockets and fumbling in bags they carried. "We don't have much to show our gratitude with," the man said, "but we wanted to give you some souvenirs to demonstrate our appreciation for your help." One by one they each gave her a simple utensil they'd used during the war.

Yet for others, liberation meant a time not for appreciation but for revenge. During the occupation of Kuching the Japanese had treated the Chinese with particular harshness and had also inflamed the Malays against them. So at the end of war some Chinese attacked the Malays. Soon the two groups were killing each other. A large group of Malays gathered weapons, met in a mosque, and plotted to attack the Chinese in town. Fortunately, Allied soldiers heard about their plan and put a stop to it.

As soon as foreign mail service resumed, Joshua and Eunice lost no time in writing to family back in China. To their joy, they learned that although their families had suffered much hardship, everyone was safe. The couple immediately began making plans for a visit home.

"But first," he told his wife, "we need to get the work of the school and church back on track. They're appointing me principal again, so we'll have to round up all the teachers and get organized."

"It's almost like starting over," she sighed. "We'll have to visit the church members and encourage them to start attending again, and to send their children back to school."

Joshua immediately requested government funds to renovate damaged buildings and to get the school operating again. Then he worked to track down all the school furniture stored in different places during the war and return it to the campus. Soon the enrollment grew to such numbers that the staff had to conduct morning and afternoon sessions to accommodate all the students. In time the school developed into a bilingual school, with English language classes in the morning session and Chinese in the afternoon.

Thanks to energetic recruiting by Joshua and the other staff, the enrollment at Kuching's Sunny Hill School began to multiply.

One day in 1949, as Joshua riffled through the mail, he noticed a letter with a Malayan stamp and postmark. As he gazed at the message inside, he grew very silent. *Not now,* he thought. *Not now, Lord, when things are going so well. Aren't we entitled to a little peace and quiet for a change?*

The letter was a request from the Malay States Mission for him to go to Kuala Lumpur, the capital of Malaya, to serve as the principal of Teck Sin School.

Not a chance, Joshua decided. *This is definitely not a good time for such a move. Why should I go through the hassle of adjusting to another new school and a new environment?* Without breathing a word to Eunice, he wrote back, declining the invitation.

But the administrators—some of whom had once worked with him in Sarawak—refused to take no for an answer. Under great duress he finally decided to accept. But once again he had to face the difficult task of breaking the news to his wife. *This time,* he decided, *I'll bide my time, and try to be more diplomatic.*

"Eunice," he said one day when she was in an especially good mood. "How would you like to see Tet Chin again?" Tet Chin (Mrs. Chu), her best friend from their first days in Sarawak, had left for Malaya when her husband had transferred there as the mission treasurer.

"Tet Chin?" Eunice looked surprised. "Is she coming back for a visit?"

"No, but you'll be getting a chance to see her soon."

"How?"

"We have received a call to Kuala Lumpur, Malaya, and Tet Chin is there."

"What?"

"Eunice—"

"You can't do this to me!" she sobbed. "We've been here for more than nine years. I have found a home away from home. All my friends are here. Even the shopkeepers downtown are our close friends. Almost every family has had a child delivered by me. And what am I going to do without Mrs. Phang, my adopted mother? Soon our new baby will be born, and she has promised to take care of me."

Joshua felt torn as he watched her go through another emotional storm. Worse, he empathized with her, for he felt very much the same way after all their years here, but he could not turn back. He had already made the commitment, and now they could do nothing but pack whatever they needed and get rid of what they couldn't take with them.

It was distressing for Eunice to sort through their things for packing, deciding what to leave behind and what to take along! Every item she had collected through the years seemed essential, and everything held some special memories, but they had only a limited weight they could ship. It was an even greater heartbreak saying goodbye to their friends when they sailed for Malaya in January 1949. They felt as if they had left a great part of their hearts behind.

Arriving at their new place, they once more went through a period of adjustment. Thankfully, this time it didn't take them as long—probably because they'd gone through the experience before. Moreover, they were too busy with a new responsibility. On June 27, 1949, a son joined the family, and Eunice spent much of her time and energy caring for the premature and tiny baby. They named him Chin Keong (strong), with the hope that the weak baby would develop into a healthy child.

14

A Step Ahead of the Red Tide

HAS IT REALLY BEEN 10 years?

Reclining on an ocean liner deck chair, Joshua put his hands behind his head and interlaced his fingers.

Yes, it has. It's been 10 years since Eunice and I were on another liner like this, bound for Sarawak, sadly watching the shores of our homeland recede in the distance.

He scanned the horizon.

There it is—Hong Kong harbor, he mused. *I'm finally coming home to China. It's going to be great to see my relatives again.*

The year was 1949. His China visit was actually a side trip on the way to Philippine Union College. The Malay States Mission—who'd asked him to be principal of Teck Sin School in Kuala Lumpur, Malaya—had awarded him a scholarship to complete his college degree. The 1937 Sino-Japanese War and then the call to Sarawak had interrupted his college education.

Even though seeing Hong Kong's harbor made him happy, Joshua couldn't totally shake off the cloud of gloom that always lurked at the edges of his mind when he was away from Eunice and the two children. It would be a solo homecoming for him. In order for him to concentrate on his studies, he'd sent his little brood to Vietnam to live with his younger brother, Yun Ping, and family.

His thoughts turned to his relatives. The past 10 years had been tough for a loyal son and brother. During the four war years all mail service had ceased, and therefore he had had no contact with the family. And when mail finally began to arrive, it made him even more homesick for the familiar faces.

But some of those faces would be absent. The sight of the mountains around Hong Kong harbor brought the same heart-pang he'd felt in 1940 on receiving the news that his youngest brother had died when the plane he was riding in had flown into one of these very mountains during bad weather.

And another face would be absent from this reunion. Joshua's worst fear—the one that had chilled him a decade before when he had bade his father goodbye—had come true. A few years after that farewell, his father had passed away, with only three of his 12 children by his side. With the war in full force, Joshua had been unable to go home to attend his funeral and pay his last respects.

He sighed, thinking how differently things might have turned out had he stayed at home. *But at least now I have my country back,* he told himself. *The Sino-Japanese War had been at its height when I left. Now it is over, and peace has returned to China.*

Later he would think about that optimism and sigh.

As the ocean liner steamed slowly into the harbor, tears of joy welled up in his eyes. Picking up his luggage, he raced down the gangplank, his heart beating so hard that it threatened to jump out of his rib cage. He had a strong desire to kiss the oily boards of the dock, hug the sweaty dockworker nearest him, and cry out, "I'm home! I'm home!" However, he restrained himself sufficiently to walk sedately on, as befitted a pastor and school administrator.

Another short boat trip from Hong Kong brought him to the mainland. His first stop was Meishian in Guangdong, to visit his sister Sue.

Will I even recognize her? he wondered. *When I left for Sarawak, she was just a kid. But now she's studying nursing at a well-known Lutheran nurses' training institute.*

"Quick, Sue," he told her after their happy reunion. "I need your help. We must go downtown to pick up some gifts for the family. I didn't take the time to get them in Hong Kong because I wanted to get here as soon as possible."

"This'll be fun," she said eagerly. "I've been so busy with my studies that I haven't been to town in ages."

"Hey," he said, grinning, "you've been working too hard. Let's grab the next bus."

As they entered the city, Joshua stared around him. "I guess I've been away too long. I thought this city was a sleepy backwater. Things feel—different, somehow."

Her eyebrows had a worried little furrow between them. "Things *are* different. I hate politics."

"Politics? What are you talking about?"

Instead of answering, she pointed. They'd just rounded a corner, and Joshua's stomach tightened at what he saw. The square was swarming with young men in khaki uniforms, berets, and red armbands. From a loudspeaker someone was barking political ideology, and thousands of what looked like university students were cheering shrilly.

"What on earth—who *are* these people?"

"I can't believe it," Sue said numbly. "I didn't know they would come all the way down here."

"Who?"

"The Communists."

His stomach tightened further. "Sue, this isn't good. I'd heard there was a party group in Beijing, but I didn't think anything of it. But to have them rallying here . . . I don't like this one bit."

Hastily making their purchases, they hurried back to the nursing school, packed, and left for Wuhua, their home village.

When word first arrived that Joshua would be coming home, relatives began to gather from far and near for the reunion. His mother was so eager to see her son again that she went to the bus station several hours early. And when Joshua stepped down from the bus, he wept unashamedly at the joy of seeing her again after all those years, and embraced her as if he could not let go.

For 10 days the relatives stayed on to entertain him in an air of festivity. Every once in a while he tried to work the conversation around to politics. "Why are the Communists here all of a sudden?" he asked his brother Yun Ching while they stood and munched on some dumplings beside the house.

Yun Ching grimaced. "Why do you want to talk about the Communists," he growled, "when we're celebrating your homecoming?"

"But I want to know. I thought once the Sino-Japanese situation was over, everybody would be so happy that—"

The brother sighed. "This country's changing. Dramatically. The war shook everybody up, and people don't have quite as much faith in Chiang Kai-shek and the Nationalist government as they used to."

"But to accept Communism?" Joshua shook his head. "That's crazy."

"OK, so we're crazy. You haven't been here, so you don't know what we've gone through. The war got everybody really weary, and a lot of people were ripe for a change. And the Communists just slithered in and took advantage."

"But how?"

"Guerrilla bands. Propaganda units. They're everywhere, especially in the rural areas, where people are really hurting. And in the university towns, to incite all the gullible students who already know who Karl Marx was." Yun Ching glanced nervously northward. "He's coming. It won't be long until he's here."

"Who's coming? Karl Marx is dead."

"Mao Zedong. And when he gets here, he'll find that a lot of his tough young Communist cadets have softened up the ground for him. You probably saw them roaming through the village."

Joshua nodded. "At the bus stop. But look. I'm going to have to get Mother out of the country."

His brother shuddered. "You may be right."

"She's all alone in the house here, and you're working 600 miles away. And the rest of the family is either married or far away like you. I'm going to send Mom to Vietnam to be with Eunice and Yun Ping."

"May I go too?"

Joshua stared at him. "You really think it's that bad then."

"Please, my brother. Please let me go with you too."

Joshua waited until his mother was alone before breaking the news.

"I cannot go," she said in distress. "This has been my home for years. The only other homes I've ever known have been the ones on school campuses where your father taught."

"Mama, remember the Japanese war? The Communists will be worse than the Japanese!"

"I cannot bear the thought of leaving Sue behind," Mother continued.

"She is my youngest daughter, and she is still single. And she hasn't graduated from nursing school yet."

"Mama, that's not important right now. What's important is—"

"And I would be afraid to be trapped in the cabin of a ship all those days on the ocean."

"Boats are *safe,*" her son insisted.

"But what if I get seasick?" she demanded. "You know that I can get sick just riding on a bus."

"Mama," he said intently, "I want you to be safe. Remember how you always called me your favorite son?"

She put her head in her hands.

"I've been separated from you for 10 years," he continued. "You're in your 70s now. I can't bear the thought of never seeing you again if I let you stay behind. And don't you want to see your two grandchildren overseas before you die?"

Over the next few days her relatives and friends labored with her. Finally she agreed. "I will go," she said, "but on one condition: that Sue comes with us too."

"Mama, you have made the right decision," Joshua said with relief. Sue was agreeable too. Her relatives' dire predictions about life under Communism had made an impression on her.

Together with Joshua, Sue, and Yun Ching, Mother left the village amid a lot of crying and lingering farewells, her children and grandchildren and other relatives grieving to think that they might never see her again.

From Wuhua they went back to the campus of the nursing school. Now it was Sue's turn to ride an emotional roller coaster. "Joshua," she said at one point out of their mother's earshot, "why did you have to agree to Mother's condition that I go with you?"

He stared at her in dismay. "Sue, you said you would! You're not having second thoughts, are you?"

"I'm in love," she said simply.

His jaw fell. "You're *what?* But you never mentioned any boyfriend!"

"I'm in love with this *campus!* I have been ever since I first set foot on it. I've got many good friends here. I love these modern, magnificent buildings, and the nurses' quarters are the best you can find anywhere. My classes are interesting and challenging."

"That won't mean a thing with Mao breathing down your neck."

"Joshua, in three more months I'll graduate. I'll finally get that certificate I've dreamed about and worked so hard for. It's my passport to my career. And it would be stupid to abandon it just because you think I need to be in Vietnam."

Joshua cleared his throat. A firm, elder-brotherly frown began to gather on his face.

"Don't you look at me like that," she snapped. "There's another reason I'm staying."

"So it's a boyfriend after all?"

"No, it's not a boyfriend. This school's German and Swiss administrators are leaving."

The frown intensified. "Of course they're leaving. And you know why. The Communists are going to make it tough on foreigners with any sort of high position."

"That may be, but because of my efficient work, they have handpicked me to be the hospital's new treasurer. And they've already started training me. So what would be the harm of staying just three more months? If worse came to worse, I can always leave for Vietnam after I get my certificate."

"Think back to the reunion," he urged her. "Remember how everybody predicted dark and perilous days ahead if the Communists were to take complete control of the country? Remember how the relatives told us to get out, or we'd regret it the rest of their lives? You think you'll be safe as hospital treasurer? Anybody who has any connections with any foreign organization will be in peril. Didn't you see what was happening at the railroad station as we arrived—those crowds of people waiting to buy tickets? If we wait any longer, we might be stuck right here!"

But Sue kept dragging her feet. Joshua was getting more desperate as the days slipped by. How could he convince her?

"Sue, let's pray about this," he finally said.

She agreed, and they took the matter to God and pleaded with Him for guidance.

And as if simply waiting for their prayers, the Lord provided not only a solution but great encouragement to go along with it. The brother and sister went to see both the hospital administrator and the nursing school director with a special request—to let Sue take her final exams three months early. Both officials were sympathetic, but said that they would have to take the matter to a committee. "We've got to make sure that we don't set a precedent with this," they said, "but your grades have been excellent, and we know that you would have no problem at all passing the exams."

The committee met and was warmly supportive—and also urgent in their advice. "Leave the country now," its members said. "We won't require you to take the final exams, because we know you have the material mastered already. After graduation we'll send you your certificate." Delighted, Sue and her brother praised God for His "more than we ask or think" response.

Once she had made her decision, Joshua found himself with another big hurdle to clear. He'd deposited the bulk of his money in Hong Kong and had entered China with only enough cash to buy gifts for his family and then pay for his ticket to the Philippines. But when he arrived in Guangzhou, he discovered that since the Communists had taken over the province, what little he had left in Hong Kong currency was obsolete, and he was penniless.

Somehow they were able to find barely enough money to purchase boat tickets for the four of them to Swatou, the last bastion of the retreating Nationalist army. To get the passage for his family to go on to Vietnam, he had to set out in faith, trusting in God to work a miracle for them. Surely He would not fail him now, seeing that He had performed so many miracles for them in the past.

What happened in Swatou over the next few days had all the excitement of an action movie. First, Joshua had to get everyone inoculated, and he managed to persuade a doctor friend to give them the shots without charge. Then he raced around to see a couple friends to take out a loan to buy tickets and other necessities. "As soon as I get back to my bank in Hong Kong I'll reimburse you," he pleaded. His friends were exceptionally kind and generous, immediately lending him $500. Relieved, he set out for the office of the shipping company, only to encounter another setback.

"Sorry," the shipping official said. "We can't take cash. The Communists will be here in just a few days, and your money won't be worth the paper it's printed on."

"But how can I pay you?" Joshua sputtered.

"With rice."

Stumbling out of the shipping company office, Joshua desperately racked his brain for a solution. *Where am I going to get large quantities of rice before our tickets expire?* he asked himself. *I don't know the area.*

Suddenly he remembered an old friend from his home village who now operated a grocery store in Swatou.

"You're in luck," the friend announced after they finished their greetings and he learned the reason for Joshua's visit. "In the past few months the price of rice has been exceptionally high in view of the impending Communist takeover. But now it has suddenly dropped! You'll be able to pay for your tickets and still have quite a bit of cash left over for yourself."

With a great sense of relief Joshua put his mother, brother, and sister on the ship to Vietnam—and just in time. The harbor was swarming with refugees scrambling to get on the ship and filling the cabins to overflowing. The ship was so packed that Joshua feared it might sink, but at least his family were on board.

"Thank You, heavenly Father, for Your great kindness," he prayed. "Thank You for keeping us just steps ahead of the Red forces, and getting us out of the country in time. Now I can sail on to the Philippines to continue my studies."

However, his classwork this time would not be clear sailing. Joshua loved learning, but it had been 11 years since he'd been in school. And as he enrolled in Philippine Union College, he faced a still more formidable hurdle: the school taught all classes in English.

In Sarawak he'd picked up a little of the language, but nothing had prepared him for the huge vocabulary he needed to understand his lectures. *This is really frustrating,* he fumed inwardly. *I've got to spend hours and hours doing my assignments—and I'm having to read my textbooks again and again to comprehend their contents. And oh, how I miss my family.*

To save his sanity he had to talk firmly to himself. *I'm really fortunate,* he would say. *I didn't have to take remedial English like many of the other foreign students. How I passed the writing proficiency test I'll never know. It was probably a miracle.*

Perhaps the subject he'd chosen for his essay had helped. He had related his dramatic escape from death during the Sarawak's Japanese occupation. The story was so exciting that it's possible that the testing service staff took pity on him.

So Joshua did his best to enjoy his college experience. Through the gradually clearing fog of the English language he discovered that each class he attended was informative and stimulating and gave him a wealth of material on evangelism.

After he had been at the college for some time, he discovered a Chinese Adventist church in Quezon City near Manila. He immediately started attending and found that its members included some of his former pastors, teachers, or schoolmates from China. The friendliness of one of the elders, David Dee, especially impressed him.

"Why don't you spend every weekend in my home?" David asked him. "That way you can attend Sabbath services and then help with visitation and Bible study in the afternoon."

"I'd love to," Joshua responded gratefully.

"I've got an idea," Dee said one Sabbath afternoon.

"What's your idea?"

"You know Dr. Nelson's prison ministry program?"

Joshua nodded. Some time back, Philippine Union College president A. N. Nelson had begun a prison ministry for the Japanese POWs. After several months 18 of them had requested baptism. Then a ministry for Filipino inmates was organized, leading to more than 100 baptisms.

"Why don't we start a prison ministry for Chinese inmates?" David continued.

Joshua's eyes widened. "Let's do it. That is, assuming that there are enough Chinese to work with."

The two men immediately approached the prison's director and learned that the Chinese population numbered more than 100. Soon 30 or 40 began attending the Sabbath afternoon services. David and Joshua studied the Voice of Prophecy lessons with them and taught them how to sing, pray, and read the Bible. After a few months nearly a dozen joined the church.

Then something most interesting happened.

At the very first meeting two of the inmates had stood out from the rest. Toh and Chua were especially helpful and demonstrated leadership abilities. They volunteered to pass out the Voice of Prophecy lessons and did their best to quiet the others down when they became too noisy. But after the first meeting Toh stopped attending.

"Joshua," David said one day, "something's bothering me."

His friend glanced at him alertly. "What's wrong?"

"Toh's voice sounded extremely familiar to me."

"You must have a good memory for voices," Joshua said. "I don't even remember it. And he hasn't come back since that first meeting."

"I know that voice," David repeated. "Very, very well."

"Well, was his face familiar too?"

"No. That's what's so strange. You'd think that if his voice was familiar, his face would be too. But it's not."

"Interesting," Joshua said thoughtfully.

For days afterward David Dee's thoughts returned again and again to Toh's voice. Then, just when he was ready to give up, it finally hit him.

"I've got it!" he told Joshua excitedly the next time they met. "Remember how I told you about the time I was kidnapped?"

Joshua's jaw fell. "Yes, I remember."

One day David had just emerged from his car when a group of rough-looking strangers surrounded him and shoved him back inside. He fought frantically, but they outnumbered him. Blindfolded and helpless, he sensed himself being driven to an unknown hideout. Since he was one of Manila's wealthier residents, the men had kidnapped him for ransom.

"And as I sat there in the darkness," David continued, "I kept hearing this voice. It was the voice of my guard."

Joshua's eyes widened. "So Toh was guarding you, and you never saw his face."

"I'm almost sure of it. And that's why he never came back to the meetings. He recognized me. Next time we go to the prison I'm going to try to confirm it."

The following Sabbath afternoon David pulled Toh's friend Chua off to the side and asked him about it.

"I know nothing," Chua said, his face impassive. David approached the issue from several directions, but the man still refused to speak.

"Look," David finally said, "I'm not going to cause any trouble when the truth comes out. I just want to know, that's all."

Chua stared into Dee's face for a long time. Finally he nodded. "It is as you say. Toh is guilty and afraid. That is why he has not returned."

"Please give him my promise that, as God is my witness, I will not seek retribution. Ask him to come back to the meetings."

After Chua relayed the message, a cautious Toh once more began attending. And David and Joshua were overjoyed when Toh and Chua and several other inmates were eventually baptized.

One day David phoned Joshua. "Bad news," he said. "I just got word from Toh and Chua that they'll be executed soon."

"No!" Joshua exclaimed.

But it was true. David had learned that both Chua and Toh had been the ringleaders of the kidnapping gang. It had snatched many other wealthy Chinese businessmen besides David in Manila and the surrounding areas. However, their kidnapping spree had come to an abrupt end when they kidnapped the eldest son of one of the richest local Chinese tycoons and asked for 1 million Philippine pesos in ransom.

The victim, however, was able to bribe one of the guards and send a message to his father, giving him the location of his kidnappers' hideout. The police stormed the place and rescued the young man, and Chua and Toh, being leaders of the group, received life imprisonment.

After having been in prison for some time, the two decided to launch a legal appeal to have their sentences reduced. Ironically, instead of shortening their prison term, the appellate judge invoked the death sentence on them. "You asked for the biggest kidnapping ransom in the history of this country," he said. "I am going to make an example of you as a warning to other kidnappers."

Immediately Joshua and David began a round of visits to the prison director, the court officials, and even the mayor of the city in a desperate attempt to stay the execution. But the date had been set, and the judge was immovable. A desperate Toh renounced his Adventist faith and joined the Catholic Church, whose bishop had promised to get him pardoned.

Chua, however, remained a true Seventh-day Adventist till the end. Joshua and David could do nothing but to prepare him for the execution by providing him with the assurance of the Bible promises of an eternal life beyond. In the days prior to the execution they did a lot of praying with him.

The day for the execution came, and both David and Joshua had the heartbreaking experience of watching as guards led both Chua and Toh (whose bishop had been unable to save him) into the execution chamber and strapped them to the electric chair. Throughout the ordeal, however, they were deeply moved and comforted by the look of peace and confidence on Chua's face. They saw him bow his head in prayer before he took his place on the chair. At a signal from the prison guard, the executioner turned the current on, and a shudder went through Chua's body. Then he slumped in his chair, and a few minutes later someone pronounced him dead.

While mourning his death, his two spiritual mentors found themselves comforted by the thought that he was ready to go to his rest until his Savior resurrected him to a life free from sin. From this painful experience Joshua recognized the need to reach all kinds of people with his ministry, and he better understood that Christ's grace can touch even the greatest of sinners.

15

In Active Service

No," Eunice said.

Joshua sighed. He'd known it wasn't going to be easy.

"No," she repeated. "You've done this to me once too often."

Having graduated from Philippine Union College in 1951, Joshua had joined his family in Singapore. Just before his return, Eunice and Mary had moved there from Vietnam, and they now considered Singapore home, since all church activity on mainland China had shut down after the Communist takeover. Armed with new knowledge and materials for evangelism acquired from his two years of training, Joshua felt more ready than ever to spread the gospel.

He'd hoped that the mission would station him in Singapore. But its leadership wanted him to care for a bilingual congregation in Ipoh, Malaya. And now he found himself facing yet another family conference.

His wife was close to tears. "So you're honestly going to drag us off to another new country?" she demanded. "We've just gotten used to Singapore. I've just unpacked our things and bought some new furniture. Do you mean to tell me we'll just have to pack up again?"

"But you haven't bought a *lot* of things," he said in a voice he hoped sounded consoling. "It'll be easier to pack now than it would have been later."

"And what about my job?" Now a nurse at Youngberg Memorial Hospital, she brought in a good income. "And I've just made some new friends. Do I have to start everything all over again?"

"And what about me?" Mary wailed.

Startled, Joshua turned to her. He'd never anticipated that his 12-year-old daughter would join the battle.

"Dad, you don't know how tough it's been for me," she said. "I'm only now starting to get better grades."

He stared at her. "What do you mean?"

"You weren't around when Mary first started school here," Eunice broke in. "All the classes are in English, not Chinese. She had forgotten all her English the two years we were in Vietnam. And she came home one day just sobbing her heart out because her grade card showed a string of F's."

"I'm sorry, sweetheart. That must have been terrible for you. However—"

"And," Eunice continued, "she slunk around the house with a totally defeated look for two whole weeks. But now she's beginning to catch on, and she's making some real progress. This is the perfect opportunity for her to get an excellent grasp of English. You need to call the mission back and tell them that now is not a good time."

She paused. When he said nothing, she gave him a puzzled glance. "Joshua? Are you listening?"

"Sorry. I was—just thinking of something." What he was thinking, though he didn't tell her right away, was something his daughter's comment had reminded him about.

My concern isn't for her grades, he told himself, *or for how the change in schools is going to affect her. Kids can adjust a whole lot more quickly than adults can. What I just remembered was that Ipoh has no Adventist church school for her grade level. That means we'll have to either put Mary in a public school there or leave her here in Singapore.*

"Let's pray," he said urgently. "Eunice, and you too, Mary. Let's pray."

Mother and daughter looked at each other and raised their eyebrows, but they nodded. *I have a feeling, though,* Eunice thought to herself, *that I'm not going to like the answer one bit.*

And once he told her of his concerns about Mary's education, she voiced her own worries. "She's only 12, Joshua. All the other boarding students in the school here in Singapore are in their late teens or older."

"Our daughter deserves a Christian education."

"She also deserves a father. You've been gone from her for two years.

And now you're announcing that you and I are going to go away and leave her."

"Eunice, just keep praying."

"I *am* praying. But there's something else you haven't thought out."

"What?"

"Finances," she said firmly. *"Money.* Unless I can somehow manage to get work, you'll be supporting a family of five. Remember, your mother is with us. And if you insist on leaving Mary here, coming up with her tuition payments is going to make it even harder."

Joshua shut his eyes. "My head hurts. I don't think that, aside from my very first call, I've ever felt so perplexed."

For days, and far into each night, Joshua and Eunice debated and agonized over the decision. They spent a great deal of time on their knees, pleading for divine guidance and strength to face the future. After a great deal of prayerful deliberation, they concluded that they must indeed go where God called them, no matter what the personal sacrifice, and that at all costs they must give their child a Christian education. As for their potential financial problems, they believed that God would provide when the time came.

When the Chongs were called to Ipoh, Malaya, they reluctantly decided to leave 12-year-old Mary behind iin Singapore so she could get an Adventist Christian education. She loved the school so much that she did literature evangelist work in Ipoh during vacations, and earned full scholarships plus extra spending money to continue attending school in Singapore.

"Smile, Eunice," Joshua said in a not-too-steady voice.

Side by side, they leaned out the window of a slowly moving railway car and waved goodbye to their daughter.

"I'm going back," Eunice suddenly announced with a catch in her voice. "I'm not leaving my daughter alone. The train's going slowly enough. I can still jump off in time."

Joshua put his arm around his wife. "She'll be all right. Smile. Let the last thing she sees be your smile."

But as soon as Mary was out of sight, Mom, Dad, Grandma, and little brother sobbed together in their railway compartment. All the way to their new home they felt a great void in their hearts.

And at first their new home didn't add much joy to those hearts. Their new surroundings sobered even the ever-optimistic Joshua.

"We've been spoiled," he said to Eunice.

She nodded. "Singapore does that to a person." Glancing around her, she said, "It's as if we're back in the 1800s."

The Ipoh church was a bare wooden structure. Inside, a rough partition divided the room into a church sanctuary area and a one-room school for a few first- and second-grade students.

Their house was simple too—another spare wooden structure with a zinc roof. When it rained, and it rained heavily there, they felt as if they were being pelted by hail. It was hard enough to live in an old house in the middle of nowhere. But the interior did not in any way resemble a home. Because they had to leave their furniture behind in Singapore and had no money to buy new furniture after paying for Mary's tuition, they had to make do with cardboard boxes and wooden crates as tables and chairs.

All around them sprawled a jungle of banana plants and luxuriant "flame of the forest" (a tropical tree with tiny leaves and scarlet blossoms year-round). Bananas grew everywhere, and the very name of the area of Ipoh where they lived, Kampong Pisang, meant "banana village." Beyond the banana plants rose a wall of limestone hills that seemed to shut them off from the outside world.

Since the local government hospital refused to recognize Eunice's nursing diploma, she wasn't able to supplement family income by working as a nurse. Mary's tuition, room and board, and her other Singapore expenses took half of her father's salary. That meant that Eunice had to exercise a lot of ingenuity in preparing dishes that were palatable and yet filling for her family. Often she had to share them with church members who turned up unexpectedly, because, as a pastor's wife, she had to demonstrate hospitality to all. This frequently stretched their budget well beyond its limits.

One day she opened the door to admit a widower, words of appreciation pouring from his lips. "Thank you, Mrs. Chong. Thank you so much for your hospitality. I am so touched by your invitation. It means so much for me to spend this evening with your family."

"Please come in and sit down," Eunice said, trying to keep the panic from her voice. *Hospitality?* she asked herself. *Invitation? What's this man talking about? Have I forgotten some kind of party we were supposed to host?*

Then it hit her. Joshua must have invited him to their home for dinner on the eve of the Mooncake Festival. *He forgot to tell me about it,* she thought. *And now he's nowhere in sight.*

She darted a look at her dining table (the wooden crate with a small tablecloth draped over it). Not expecting guests, she'd boiled a little bean soup for supper. "Excuse me, please," she said brightly. Racing out of the door, she hurriedly gathered some vegetables from her garden and managed to cook up a meal for their unexpected guest.

"Eunice," Joshua said one day. "I've been thinking."

She glanced at him warily. When her husband talked like that, it usually meant that life would change in some dramatic—and usually unsettling—manner.

"Our finances are in a really bad way," he continued.

"They certainly are."

"I've got an idea. When Mary comes home for her year-end vacation, let's have her do literature evangelism work."

His wife's jaw fell. "Where on earth did you manage to come up with that idea?" she sputtered.

"What do you mean, 'that idea'?"

"Don't you remember how young she is? She's not even a teenager yet!"

"Come on, Eunice. Don't throw cold water on this yet. Let's let her try it."

"This hot weather is affecting your head," she told him. "Do you realize that if you attempted something like this in England or America, you'd be breaking child labor laws?"

He shrugged. "A little work never hurt anyone. You know that. After all, you worked hard when we were growing up together. So did I."

She shuddered. *Too* hard," she said firmly. "And how do you even know she'd be any good at selling books? She may not even make any money at all."

"We won't know if she doesn't try."

Eunice finally gave in. "Well, I suppose we could see how she does. But just think of sending her out into that sweltering heat. Isn't she going to resent having to work during her vacation when she has been away from home most of the year?"

"I think it will be good for her. The quicker she learns a solid work ethic, the better."

"But she's not going alone," his wife said. "I'll go with her, and if I can't, then maybe some of the adult colporteurs can."

He nodded. "Fine. But make her do all the talking."

When Mary arrived home, she was surprisingly calm about the suggestion. "I guess so," she said after she'd thought it over. "Just show me how."

Two weeks later Joshua made it a point to have a conversation with his daughter. "Out with it, Mary," he said firmly.

The girl glanced around in alarm. "What's wrong, Dad?"

He grinned. "What's your secret?"

"My secret?"

"Your mom tells me you're just raking in the money. How do you do it?"

She thought for a moment. "I think it might be because I'm so young," she finally replied.

"But you're doing the talking, right?"

She nodded. "When I go into the homes or the stores, they always tell me how impressed they are that somebody my age is trying to help support the family. They say, 'You're not just frittering away your vacation time like the other kids do.' And they purchase some books. Then they call up their relatives and friends and tell them to buy some too."

And even though she was by far the youngest literature evangelist in the union—and the division—by the end of her vacation Mary had earned a full scholarship for the upcoming year and had even put aside some extra cash for her other expenses.

Now Mary looks back on that time with satisfaction. "I was initially terrified of going out to meet people," she says, "for I was an extremely shy kid at that time. But two things got me over my fears. For one thing, I never went alone. Also, I loved attending school in Singapore, and if this was what it took to raise the money, that's what I would do. And these colporteuring experiences gave me a lot of valuable training in public relations and financial management."

During the evenings Eunice did her best to get reacquainted with her daughter. "How did you feel being away from Mom and Dad for nine months out of the year?" she asked anxiously.

"I missed you all, and I cried a lot at first. But it's really not that bad. I'm getting to know a lot of interesting kids from all over Southeast Asia."

"But you're so much younger than they are."

Mary grinned. "I'm their mascot. The older students in the dorm treat me like their little sister. When they come back from vacations, they bring me gifts. They take me downtown to festivals, and the guys carry me around on their shoulders so I can get a good view of everything."

"Well, I'm glad they're treating you well," her mother said in relief.

"They're spoiling me rotten. And they even take me on dates."

Eunice hiccuped. "You're going on *dates?*"

"No, Mom," the girl giggled. "It's not like *that.* I mean, when a guy and a girl go out on a date, they take me along. As their chaperone."

Later Mary would become a teacher, and her multicultural dorm experience would prove valuable as she dealt with students from all languages and socioeconomic backgrounds. And she's kept in touch with a number of her school friends through the years, most recently by the Internet.

16

Joy and Sacrifice in Singapore

LIKE HIS WIFE AND DAUGHTER, Joshua was working hard. The little Ipoh congregation finally managed to scrape together enough money to buy a lot in the center of town and to erect a new church building. He faithfully visited both attending and nonattending members, and soon he had the church filled with the fruits of his labor.

And it was in the cracks between meetings and visits, as well as sermon preparation and building committees, that a new vision began to form in his mind.

"Eunice, I have a dream."

His long-suffering wife sighed. "I hope it involves a call that brings us closer to Mary."

"No, no call yet."

"Well, what's your dream?"

"I'm convinced," he said, "that we need more Chinese ministers."

She nodded. "They're few and far between these days."

Everywhere in Southeast Asia—the Philippines, Sarawak, Singapore, Malaya, and in other countries—there were Chinese congregations. But China's new closed-door policy blocked any pastors from emerging from that country. The Southeast Asia Union Mission did operate a college that trained ministers, but only in English, and few from mainland China had any exposure to it.

"I'm going to start praying about this," Joshua announced. "I am living proof that a mission school not only nurtures church members but converts nonmembers."

Three years later, in 1954, the opportunity came for turning his vision into reality. "Eunice! Come and look at this letter!"

She eyed the envelope cautiously. "Where to now?"

He grinned. "What do you mean, where to now?"

"It's a call," she said. "I can tell."

"It's a call," he agreed.

"And from the fact that you don't have a guilty look on your face, it must be one you think I'll like."

Laughing, he gathered her into his arms. "We're going back to Singapore!"

"Joshua! No! Really?" Now it was she who was hugging him. "We'll be back with Mary again? All year?"

"All year."

"What do they want you to do?"

"Pastor-teacher," he said.

"Well, that's nothing new."

Soon they were back in Singapore, reunited with Mary, and during the next several years (including two at what would later be Andrews University earning a graduate degree) Joshua would see many of his dreams fulfilled.

The Singapore Chinese church had just relocated to a magnificent building donated by a wealthy church member who was also one of the Chongs' friends from Sarawak days. As soon as Joshua got a glimpse of the basement's several multipurpose rooms, his imagination took flight. In his mind he saw the rooms turned into classrooms filled with students. He immediately worked together with the Chinese church to found what would become San Yü High School, Singapore's first Chinese-language secondary school.

"Let's open enrollment to non-Adventists as well," he urged the planning committee. "I want to make this a mission school."

"That's a good idea," someone said, "but what are we going to do for money?"

"It's going to be tough," another committee member chimed in. "The Malay States Mission is already operating an English elementary and high school, and they don't have a budget big enough for us."

But the church members didn't flinch. Rising to the challenge, they set about soliciting funds from the public. Enrollment grew, and soon the school needed new buildings and more teachers, so the board bought the next-door plot of ground owned by the Far Eastern Division and had a new building constructed.

But some on the board were concerned.

"We can't simply rely on the public for the funds to support the school year after year," they said. "Let's come up with a more dependable source of income."

They finally found it in a "fun fair" the school held one year.

"The community loves fairs," board members said. "Let's do one every year, and make it even larger so that we can attract more people. Not only will this boost our operating fund, but it'll be good publicity for the school."

"And let's have a Jumble Sales Day," someone else suggested.

And it was Jumble Sales Day (what Americans would call a rummage sale) that proved to be the most popular event. Several months in advance church members, faculty, and students turned out in force to solicit donations from local stores and restaurants—food items, furniture, clothes, shoes, household utensils, and anything else that people might want to buy. They also carried books of tickets with them, selling them as they went.

Joshua (right) loved learning as much as teaching. Here he is, along with Pastor James Wang (who'd served as principal of Singapore's San Yü Adventist High School) on their graduation day at Andrews University, where Joshua earned his master's degree.

On the day of the jumble sale, the school pitched a huge tent on the sports field and converted the grounds into a bazaar. People gathered on the campus and strolled through the bazaar to enjoy a variety of local food and drinks before going through the stalls to snap up the donated goods. Over time, this annual event earned the school huge profits.

Even after the Singapore government acquired the campus of the English Adventist School operated by the mission and the English-language school merged with San Yü High School, it continued—and continues—to thrive on annual jumble sale funds.

In time, devout church members, catching the vision for expanding the school, supported it in other ways. Some included it in their wills. Others created memorial funds to honor the deaths of parents and other relatives. "Surely," Joshua often said, "the Lord has blessed the efforts of the people to promote and support Christian education in unprecedented ways."

Joshua's mother, Mei Hwa, lived to the ripe old age of 94. Here she is, seated in a 1960s-era family photo. Behind her, from left: Dayton, Joshua, Eunice, Joshua's sister Sue, and Mary.

The Chongs' little son, to whose Chinese name they'd added the English first name of Dayton, provided them with much joy—and comic relief—during these busy times. As a premature baby (4.5 pounds at birth), he'd been as tiny as a kitten, and his cry actually sounded like that of a kitten. Even at age 4 he was tiny for his age, but he eventually grew big and strong.

From the first, Dayton found himself mesmerized by his dad's dynamic preaching. His sister, Mary, has vivid memories of him acting out Bible characters wearing one of his mother's robes and with a bath towel wrapped turbanlike around his head. Then he would "play preacher," seating the 2-year-old daughter of a family friend in front of him and preaching into a toy microphone while standing behind a pulpit made from a crate. When he later became a pastor, everyone noticed that he was like his father in every way—in his dedication to his church members and the dynamic way he presented his messages.

"I've often wondered, though," Mary recalls, "why Dayton still wanted to be a pastor after what he went through as a PK. In spite of his tiny size, he was a really active kid, and he found it especially difficult to keep still in church. During Sinagpore church services he would break free and race around on the sidewalks outside the building. One of the elders always took it upon himself to report Dayton's pranks to Pastor Joshua. And when the family arrived home from church, Dad would administer a spanking. Poor Dayton—he got spanked a lot. Yet I believe that ever since he was a little boy, he had no other ambition except to be a pastor just like his dad."

Though working with San Yü School was exciting, Joshua hadn't forgotten his other dream. He began to pour out his heart to the visionary P. G. Miller, president of the Malayan Union Seminary (later named Southeast Asia Union College).

"We need college-level ministerial training in the Chinese language," he told Miller. "Our Chinese churches need pastors."

Ever the teacher, Joshua loved making evangelistic series learning experiences for students. He even got his family members involved in this 1963 series in Muar, Malaya. His son, Dayton, is second from the left; Joshua's wearing the black coat in the center; Mary is next to him; and her husband, David, is on the far right.

Miller didn't hesitate. Knowing Joshua's reputation for tenacity, the seminary president formed a new Chinese training department and added it to the curriculum.

"All right," he told Joshua, "I'm giving you what you want. And I'm appointing you program director—but for now, you'll have to be the sole instructor for all the courses!"

Joshua advertised the program widely in Chinese churches all over Southeast Asia, and soon drew students from not only from Singapore but also Borneo, Vietnam, Thailand, and Malaya. Capitalizing on his close connections with Singapore's Chinese church, he was able to give his students immediate field experience. They taught Sabbath school classes, led youth programs, and put their homiletics class training to work preaching in the main church, as well as branch churches throughout Singapore. During their vacation he helped them conduct evangelistic series.

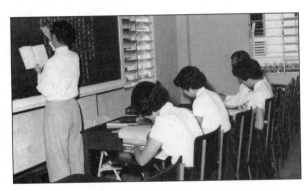

China's closed-door policy caused a shortage of Chinese-speaking pastors in Southeast Asia. The Malayan Union Seminary classes were in English only, but at Joshua's urging, the president formed a new Chinese training department. Here students diligently copy Joshua's blackboard notes.

Joshua also took special interest in the personal lives of the young people under his care. As a pastor he recognized how important it was that future ministers find the right mates. At least three pairs of his students formed life unions and were able to work together in the churches they later pastored.

His interest in his students continued even into his retirement years, when he taught theology at Taiwan Adventist College from 1981 to 1984.

One day, eyes twinkling, he hurried across campus to find his daughter, who at that time was also serving as a missionary together with her husband at the school.

"Mary! Guess what!"

She had long ago developed her mother's caution about things that excited her father. Studying him carefully, she cautiously asked, "What?"

"Last night I had a dream!"

"A dream?"

"A *wonderful* dream!" he chortled, his face exuding joy and excitement. "I attended the wedding of Jane and Mark!"

His daughter's eyebrows shot up. "You mean your student Mark?"

"Of course!"

Mary rolled her eyes. "Jane and Mark? Come on, Dad, you're dreaming too much. They're not even close friends. And besides, they're dating other people."

"They're made for each other. I know it."

"Dad, you be careful now. Don't ruin things."

"Oh, don't worry about me. But I'm going to pray."

To the immense surprise of Mary and others, Mark began dating Jane almost immediately. Upon their graduation a couple years later Joshua's prophecy came true. They were married, with Mary's husband, David, officiating, and their daughter as flower girl. Today Mark is a successful pastor in Taiwan, with Jane as his effective cominister.

But Joshua was more than a matchmaker—he also modeled for his students the kind of commitment and dedication that distinguishes a minister's life. As a pastor he gave of his energy, time, and means. He was with his members when they were in pain, visiting them in the hospital to comfort them with scripture and prayer. When their loved ones died, he grieved with their families, consoling them with promises of hope and life. With great caring and concern he helped resolve family conflicts—and even helped people move, then came to bless their new dwellings.

And he ministered with his money, too—something that caused his family to tremble. He was a tireless promoter for evangelism and other charitable needs—and especially for major projects such as the San Yü High School foundation. "To show how important I think this project is," he would declare from the front, "I'm going to personally donate—" and then he'd mention a sum that would cause Eunice to stifle a gasp. He lent cash to members who'd failed in business, to tide them over and to help them get started again. Constantly digging deep into his pocket to give to those in need, he'd often find that pocket empty before the end of most months.

One day, as his car stopped at an intersection waiting for the light to change, a professional beggar approached him and asked for money. Obediently Joshua pulled out his wallet and spread it open. When the beggar saw the single remaining bill, he laughed scornfully. "Forget it," he sneered. *"I've* got more money than you have!" Then he turned and strode off.

"Joshua, you've simply got to be more sensible with our funds," Eunice often told him. "Our children are getting to be college age, and you know how much a college education costs."

To this he always answered: "God has said, 'Give, and it will be given to you' [Luke 6:38]." After that, Eunice could do nothing but try to catch his faith in God to provide when the time came. She did live, however, to see the fulfillment of this promise—her children were indeed able to complete their college and graduate education with scholarships God provided.

Needless to say, the years Joshua spent carrying the load of both a church and a school began to take their toll, sometimes in frightening ways.

One evening, after an especially taxing school board meeting, three of its members got into his van with him. Together they rode along, still deep in debate about the unresolved agenda items. "Watch out!" one of them suddenly shouted.

Joshua had missed seeing a red light at an intersection and driven straight through it. With a loud screech and a terrific bang, a car coming from the left struck the van and sent it spinning and somersaulting. The impact violently threw Joshua and his passengers around inside.

The van finally came to rest on its roof, its window glass smashed. Concerned passersby hurried over and peered inside, expecting to see mangled bodies. As they examined the wreck, its passengers stirred one by one and slowly wriggled out through the windows. As they brushed away shards of glass, onlookers noticed only minor bruises. Even the police could not comprehend how four people did not get killed in such a bad accident. "They must have nine lives," the stunned spectators commented, but Joshua firmly believed that God had performed a miracle to save him and his passengers.

The second accident occurred on a Sabbath afternoon. Even though Sabbath is supposed to be a day of rest, being an Adventist pastor made it Joshua's busiest. He began the day by making the rounds with the van to pick up elderly church members and transport them to the services. Then, after teaching the Sabbath school lesson and preaching the sermon in the main church, he hastily gulped down some potluck food and drove his ministerial students to branch churches in other parts of the island to conduct afternoon meetings.

This particular Sabbath was even more taxing, because his usual hectic week had included a strenuous board meeting. With his students in the back of the van mumbling their sermons over to themselves, an exhausted Joshua dozed off at the wheel.

Suddenly a series of loud clatters and bumps jolted him back awake. His eyelids flew open just in time to see a massive lamppost racing to meet him. Desperately he swerved to avoid contact with it. Too late—the van rammed into the side of the post with a loud crash and came to a standstill. A big crowd of passersby raced to the scene of the accident to render first aid. Again, the passengers climbed out one by one unhurt, praising God for His deliverance from what could have been a fatal accident.

In 1976 Joshua turned 65. He'd given more than 40 years to his church, at least 37 of them devoted to missions—expanding and advancing the church in mostly Southeast Asian countries. He would have con-

Joshua stands in front of the van he piloted through two serious Singapore accidents. Thanks to divine providence, all passengers survived uninjured.

tinued to work tirelessly for the Lord had he not suffered a couple minor strokes that made it necessary for him to retire from active service.

Even then, the God who had performed so many miracles in his life granted him yet another miracle to save him from permanent disability. He recovered sufficiently to work for three years at Taiwan Adventist College before moving in 1992 from Singapore to his final home in San Jose, California. But even then he continued to mentor and help with Chinese evangelism until his death.

17

Escape From Vietnam

Usually Joshua was a personal participant in his family's adventures, working and praying through various challenges on the spot. This chapter—whose events happened in 1975—tells of a time he had to watch helplessly from a distance, desperately interceding in prayer.

"EUNICE!"

From the kitchen of their Singapore home she heard Joshua's shout, followed immediately by the sound of crumpling paper. She peered around the doorway into the living room and saw her husband pacing like a caged tiger.

"What?" she asked. "What's wrong?"

His foot brushed against the ball of newspaper he'd just crushed between his fingers. Impatiently he kicked it away and kept pacing. "We've got to *do* something!" he said.

She glanced at the newspaper. "Bad news from Vietnam?"

"Right. America's pulling out for sure." He grabbed for the newspaper ball, spread it apart, and peeled the sheets away until he came to the one he wanted. "Listen to this: 'With the decision of the U.S. administration to withdraw its military presence from Vietnam, the Communist North is losing no time in advancing on the South. . . . The North is already at the gates of Saigon. The American military is making urgent preparations to evacuate the embassy.'"

Eunice drew in a trembling breath. More than two decades before, while Joshua had been attending school in the Philippines, she and her two children had stayed in Vietnam with Joshua's brother Yun Ping and his family. Though Yun Ping had passed away, his wife and family still lived there. And now—April 1975—the long, weary Vietnam War was in its last ugly spasms. As the armies of North Vietnam advanced south, they made it very clear that they would treat as enemies anybody whom they even remotely considered America's friend.

"We've got to get the family out of there somehow," he moaned. "There's not a chance that the Communists will consider them neutrals." From 1969 until 1972 his nephew Michael had worked for the U.S. Navy. Joshua's sister-in-law and nieces had served as teachers in the Adventist mission school in Cholon—and therefore also had links to the Americans.

"How much gold have you collected?" Eunice asked.

Joshua's shoulders sagged. "It's like a kidnapper's ransom. The Vietnamese boat owners are demanding 12 ounces of gold per person as passage out of the country. I've been doing what I can to scrape money together. But I'm just a poor pastor."

His breath caught in a sob, and soon the two were kneeling by the couch, weeping and praying together. "Lord," Joshua cried, "please provide a way of escape for my relatives the way You did for my mother and my family years ago!"

A few days later word came that Saigon had fallen. And like a curtain, a news blackout suddenly descended. *What is the fate of my brother's family?* Joshua wondered, and he and Eunice continued their desperate prayers.

Earlier that fateful April Joshua's nephew Michael made a frantic visit to several people in the Navy office in Saigon. "Is there any chance," he asked, "that I could be evacuated as a former employee?"

"Sorry," came the reply. "There's no plan to evacuate anyone but current employees—and it's going to be risky for them, too." One official handed him a form. "Fill this out, with your address and contact number just in case the brass decide to evacuate others, too. But don't hold your breath—there are thousands of people surging through the different government offices trying to find a way out of here."

Then came the April 21 bombshell that destroyed all hope of holding off the Communists around the city: President Nguyen Van Thieu broadcast his final speech on television, resigned his presidency, and fled to Taiwan.

On April 22 the last commercial airline flight left Saigon. Now—except for paying the boat owners' ransom and taking one's chances on the open sea—the only way out was through the American airbase. Operation Frequent Wind began, which was the signal for the American embassy to put its own evacuation plans into immediate effect. The U.S. military airlift roared into life at Tan Son Nhut air base.

Michael, his mother, and his sisters Audrey and Alice were in despair. Everything seemed hopeless. But then a wondrous series of miracles began, starting with a knock at the door.

"Mrs. Liao, please come in," Mother invited. Their visitor was a widow who lived in the apartment next door.

"Is Michael here? Oh, I am so glad," Mrs. Liao said breathlessly. "Michael, would you be so kind as to be my translator when I go see Mr. Chuck Hansberger tonight? You remember that my daughter married an American and went to live in the U.S.? My son-in-law has called Mr. Hansberger to help get me out of the country."

"Sure," Michael said. "Let's go."

Arriving at the Hansberger residence, the two discovered that the American was still at the air base working on the evacuation. Michael managed to contact him by telephone. "Tell Mrs. Liao not to worry," Hansberger said. "Arrangements have already been made for her. She'll be leaving in a few days."

As Michael hung up the phone, he noticed the Hansbergers' chauffeur waiting to speak to him. "Do you see this document?" the man said. "It's an official evacuation order for my family and me. I understand that you, along with your mother and two sisters, would like to leave. I could add your names to this paper—for a fee. That's the only way you're going to get past the American guards at the air base checkpoint."

Michael glanced at Mrs. Liao, who wore a disapproving expression. She pulled him aside and shook her head. "No," she said. "I would suggest that you work things out with Mr. Hansberger instead."

Returning home, Michael began phoning the official's house at all hours, but could reach only the housekeeper. By April 24, realizing the need for desperate measures, he phoned again.

"I have an idea," he told the housekeeper. "Would you permit my family and me to stay there tonight so that we can be sure of seeing Mr. Hansberger when he returns from the base?"

Even in peacetime it would have been highly unusual for a housekeeper to let strangers she'd met only briefly stay at her employer's house without his permission. And this was war—with the enemy occupation just hours away. Yet the woman agreed, and Michael and his family lost no time in getting to the house before the 8:00 p.m. curfew.

"Michael, look," his mother said as they stood on the Hansberger doorstep. "We're right across the street from Saigon Adventist Hospital."

Later that evening Michael began pacing nervously, waiting for Mr. Hansberger's arrival, when he suddenly heard the blaring of sirens. Glancing out the window, he saw an ambulance race into the hospital compound, while another quickly departed. "I think there's been a terrible accident," he said to the rest of the family. "I'm going to see if I can find out what happened."

He jogged across the street and peered through the gates. Hundreds of people with their luggage and personal belongings were milling around. Every time an ambulance rolled through the gates, the crowd surged forward. Michael caught sight of one of the ambulance drivers—Pastor Ralph Watts, Southeast Asia Union Mission president! Pastor Le Cong Giao, Vietnam Mission president, was charging around like a madman, trying to marshal the unruly crowd into the ambulances each time one came through the gates.

Michael's skin prickled. *They're evacuating the Adventist expatriate and national workers!* he thought. *I'm sure they're taking them to the air base to board the last planes out of the country.*

As he watched the evacuation with a mix of despair and envy, a wild idea took shape in his mind. *Time's running out,* he suddenly decided. *I can't afford to wait for Hansberger.* Dashing across the street, he hustled his mother and two sisters over into the compound. Almost immediately they spotted three young people from the Cholon Chinese church.

"We heard about the evacuation," one of them said, "and we came here to see if we could possibly join a group of evacuees."

With the help of Pastor Giao, the seven managed to waylay Pastor Watts on one of his trips back into the compound. "Please, please," they begged, "can you put our names on your list?"

Their desperation struck a sympathetic chord in the administrator. "I don't have a clue as to how I'm going to do this," he said, "but I'll try to get you out of here. Now listen carefully. Stay away from the crowd and just wait quietly at the side gate until I've gone through my list."

Filled with despair and apprehension, the seven people could only huddle beside the gate in the darkness, wondering what fate awaited them. Each time an ambulance came through the gates, they got desperately to their feet. The minutes ticked away as the crowd dwindled. Would they have a chance? As they waited, they continued to send their petitions heavenward.

Finally only a handful of people remained. Relief flooded over them as Pastor Watts looked in their direction and beckoned. They rushed to his side and scrambled into the ambulance.

It was 1:00 a.m. when the vehicle rolled through the airport gates. *Vietnam is the only home I've ever known,* Michael thought, *and now we're having to leave it.* An even deeper pang struck his heart. *And I'll probably never see Esther again.*

Esther Tran had been a special friend of his, and now that Michael's own family was assured of evacuation, his mind turned to thoughts of her welfare. She had grown up together with him and had attended the same church. The future under a Communist regime didn't promise to be exactly bright for her and her family. Her father was a millionaire, which placed them in a high-risk group.

I must get them out too! Michael thought desperately. *But how? Pastor Watts has bent over backward to accommodate us. How much further can I stretch his kindness? But I've simply got to try.*

He pulled Pastor Giao to one side. "You know the Tran Chieu family, don't you?"

The mission president nodded. "The successful businessman? I certainly do. He's on the mission's executive committee—a strong supporter of the work."

Michael shared the burden on his heart, and the pastor instantly agreed that they should make every effort to give the Trans an opportunity to evacuate. Then he went to find Pastor Watts.

"All right," Elder Watts said, "but it's going to take a bit of negotiating with the U.S. officials. And time's running out. It's 5:00 a.m. The Trans need to get here right away, because the last plane is leaving in about an hour."

Pastor Giao dashed toward the nearest phone booth.

At that moment the Trans were asleep. After several unsuccessful attempts to leave the country by boat, they'd resigned themselves to staying. The insistent ringing of the phone jarred Mr. Tran awake.

"Hello?"

"Mr. Tran, this is Pastor Giao," came the urgent voice on the other end of the line. "We have worked it out for you and your family to leave the country, but it is imperative that you get to the air base in one hour. *One hour. Do you understand?* Now I have to go." The phone went dead.

Mr. Tran rubbed his eyes. *Am I dreaming?* he wondered at first. Then the truth sank in. *Leave the country?* he thought. *How can I—*

"Get up!" he shouted to his family. "Everybody up! Kids, get dressed. Find your passports!"

As he heard his family stumbling through the house Mr. Tran's mind raced. *I can't leave Vietnam,* he thought. *I've worked so hard for what we have. If I get on that plane I'll have to leave everything behind—this huge house, our three grand pianos, all the rest of our priceless possessions. I can't go.*

"Quick!" he bellowed to his children. "I'll drive you to the airport!"

Esther and her siblings gaped at him in shocked surprise. "But what about you, Dad?"

"Your mom and I are staying. But you go. I'll be in the car."

The children glanced at each other, then turned to face their parents. "No," they said. "We're not leaving without you. You come with us, or we all stay."

A tense and painful silence followed.

Finally Mr. Tran's shoulders sagged. "All right," he said in a sad voice. "For your sakes, I'll go." He hustled his wife and children into the car, then shut the house doors for the last time. With only the clothes on their backs they bade farewell to their palatial home forever.

They arrived at the airport just before the gates closed. And as dawn came, all the evacuees were airborne, winging their way to an unknown future in the United States. As they glimpsed the fast-receding city lights below, tears flooded their eyes. Their hearts hurt as they recalled how they'd not even had time to say goodbye to relatives and friends. Yet those hurting hearts lifted in praise to God for miraculously opening doors of escape, even at the last hour.

Michael and Esther's friendship ripened into love. They married and are now the parents of two adult children.

18

Sunset and Eventide

O N JULY 14, 1999, JOSHUA sat alone in his San Jose, California, home. He'd just sent his only granddaughter off to her college summer school classes.

Dear LeAnn, he thought fondly, *my miracle child.* One day back in 1990 LeAnn had been crossing a road on her way home from school. A speeding van struck and ran over her, rolling her into the next lane, where another car rolled over the girl. The whole family was devastated, and Joshua had fasted and prayed for her recovery. Though the accident had left a gaping wound perilously close to her eye, LeAnn made a complete recovery and was back in school two months later.

Later today Joshua planned to make his daily pilgrimage to visit Eunice, his companion of more than 50 years. Some time back she had been diagnosed with multiple myeloma and was resting comfortably in a convalescent home.

His son, Dayton, was in Fresno, serving as pastor and coordinator of Asian programs for the Central California Conference. And his daughter, Mary, and son-in-law, David, were in South Korea, helping with the ministries of the Northern Asia-Pacific Division, which now included Joshua's native China.

He still remembered what a struggle he had gone through when David and Mary received that request. David had been the General Conference's associate director of youth ministries and had lived in Maryland.

Please stay close to home, his heart had cried out when David mentioned they'd be leaving for the division headquarters in South Korea. *I am so old, so feeble. Please stay close.* But like his father before him, he had ignored his own wishes.

"By all means accept this call," he'd said, forcing his famous smile into his voice. "Take God's challenge to go where your services are needed. I'm too old to go back to China and minister to my people. But I'm so thrilled and so proud to know that you two will be doing the work I always wanted to do."

Joshua and Eunice in 1990, during the celebration of Joshua's eightieth birthday.

Now Joshua sat in the comfortable silver-white love seat in the living room. On shelves all around him stood the beloved books he'd accumulated through the years. And though he was alone in the big house, and though the silence was almost overwhelming, he was not sad or lonely. He was about to begin his daily communion with his heavenly Father. It has been his practice both morning and evening to spend an hour or two reading God's Word and talking to Him.

How I treasure and relish those hours of communing with You, Father, my benefactor and deliverer, he prayed. *I have reached the ripe old age of 88, but never in all these years have I ever felt You very far from me. You have been constantly by my side, guiding me, guarding me, comforting me even in the most perilous of times and the most grievous of circumstances. You have held my hands and sustained me as I walked through the storms of life, and even "through the valley of the shadow of death." You and I have been through thick and thin together.*

As Joshua reflected on his life now, he saw how his trials and affliction had brought him closer to God. Like his earthly father before him, he had given his life to the Lord's service, accepted His call to foreign mission fields, turned to Him in times of great peril, been saved numerous times from life-threatening situations, and survived debilitating illnesses.

All his life he'd enjoyed his dual role as a minister and an educator. Now that he was no longer in active service, it was a special joy to him that his two children had taken over both roles. Dayton had been engaged in pastoral ministry ever since he had graduated from college, and Mary had been teaching in various educational institutions in Singapore, Taiwan, and the United States. The inheritance he would leave them was not great material wealth but the legacy of a life dedicated in service to the God who had sustained him.

And his students too . . . they were also serving the church as pastors or administrators in different parts of Southeast Asia. Some were even working in the South China Island Union Mission. Through them and through his children his influence had reached such places as Borneo, Malaysia, Singapore, Vietnam, Cambodia, Thailand, Hong Kong, mainland China, Korea, and even Mongolia and Japan.

Nearly 20 years before, after his two strokes, God had allowed him to recover enough to train young people in Taiwan. And even until just recently, he had visited church members with the pastor, given Bible studies, taught the Sabbath school lesson, delivered sermons in his strong and unfaltering voice, and even sung in the choir. Drawing on his vast experience, he had taken on the role of a mentor, guiding and supporting young pastors and giving them ideas and suggestions for special projects and programs to spread the Adventist message among the Chinese in America. And what was most important was that he supported them—and his children—with prayer.

Now he looked forward to attending the Central California Conference camp meeting that coming weekend. He always felt a thrill when he joined in the rousing song service or listened to the inspiring reports and sermons.

However, he was feeling tired—very tired. The Lord seemed to be saying to him, "Lie down, weary one, lie down, and I will give you rest." Still sitting on the couch with a blanket draped over his lap and legs and feeling the warmth of God's presence wrapping around him, he drifted into a restful sleep.

Then, as if from a great distance, he heard the alarmed voice of his granddaughter. "Grandpa. Grandpa, wake up. Are you OK?"

Stirring, his mind said, *I'm all right, LeAnn. I'm just tired and need to rest.* But even though his lips formed the words, he could not utter them.

Then suddenly other people filled the room, rushing around him. He felt them lifting him gently and placing him on a soft surface. Another person slid something over his nose and mouth, and he could breathe easier.

Next he realized that he was in a vehicle. Above him a siren wailed, and he remembered the air-raid sirens he had heard so long ago. But now he felt safe in the arms of his heavenly Father.

Then all grew silent as he rested on a soft bed. Struggling mightily to open one eye, he noticed his son and daughter-in-law and other relatives around him. Tears streamed down their cheeks.

It is all right, he attempted to say. *I am ready to go.* But struggle as he might, he could not get the words out of his mouth. Horrified, he realized that tubes blocked his mouth and nostrils. *I want to talk!* his mind cried, and he frantically tried to pull them out. *I want to give you my last words! I want to assure you that I am happy to be at rest, awaiting my Father's call.*

Finally he made writing gestures, and someone hurried up with pen and paper. Gripping the pen with difficulty, he scrawled on the pad, "I want to rest."

The bark of life that had taken him to so many foreign shores in mission service was now slowly bearing him to the heavenly shore. If he had been able to speak, he might have quoted Tennyson's famous poem:

> "Sunset and evening star,
> And one clear call for me!
> And may there be no moaning of the bar,
> When I put out to sea,
>
> "But such a tide as moving seems asleep,
> Too full for sound and foam,
> When that which drew from out the boundless deep
> Turns again home.
>
> "Twilight and evening bell,
> And after that the dark!

And may there be no sadness of farewell,
When I embark;

"For though from out our bourne of Time and Place
The flood may bear me far,
I hope to see my Pilot face to face
When I have crossed the bar."

A year later Eunice would follow him to her rest. Today, in the Heaven's Gate Cemetery in Los Altos, they sleep side by side awaiting their Lord's wake-up call, when He will reunite them with their loved ones and all those they were instrumental in bringing to Him.

What a day that will be!

breakfast, even though she can also be delightfully—modernly—silly at times. She washes his feet in warm, scented water and dries them with her sandal-wood scented hair. It's mostly a charming masquerade, but not entirely. Then she feeds him bits of crystallized, gingered sweets and fresh juicy fruit by hand. "Stop, stop, I'm already fat enough," he stutters in mild protest, but protests end in enough regained heat and steam to fall back into bed and dishevel and dismay Rehana again. Who says this is not "love"?

Now, Rehana knows Harish's father is an important man and rich as Midas. She also knows Harish himself is interested in the bioscope, moves in that world. She isn't hungry for his family's money, but secretly she does harbor a hope that he might get her a role in the bioscope. So many women have done it lately. All those Jewish ladies, and that Nargis, the daughter of a courtesan herself as is well-known. Why not Rehana?

Harish brings Rehana, meanwhile, costly presents, mostly jewelry that her mother Pyari Bai has intimated will be most acceptable of all gifts, except perhaps cash only. Rehana has a generous monthly allowance settled on her, his gifts not included, and she only has to ask for something for him to provide.

Involuntarily, unknowingly, Rehana begins to fantasize. Standing before the mirror while Harish fastens his newest blazing tribute around her elegant neck, she recognizes her beauty in full blaze. The fantasy begins to consume her. Why can't she be a wife? Why can't she leave this place, though the only place she knows as home, and start over again as a respectable woman? As Harish Mitter's wife?

She asks Harish in bed one night, "Will you marry me, Sahib?" She feels a chill when he says nothing but his breathing changes. She props herself up on one elbow and looks at his face, anxious and a little heated. He still doesn't speak, and she asks, as any nagging wife would do, "What? Can we not?"

"It's not done, *Jaan*," he says finally in a small voice.

Tears shoot out of her eyes. "Of course it is," she says, stomping vocally. "Suchitra from next door has just been accepted by her longtime man, and now she lives happily with him in his Bagbazaar house." Pausing, she looks at Harish aslant.

"Happily," he says, as if discovering the word for the first time.

"Yes, happily," she returns it to him like a gingerly held newborn. "Why not? Am I less than her? Because I'm from this swamp, am I less than the fancy lotuses you grow in your vast reservoirs?" She means wives. Then she flounces down on her side of the bed, wrestling with the physical pain she feels. He lies still, staring up at darkness, overcome with remorse. He can't tell her that the man who has taken Suchitra is a petty cooking oil merchant and far freer than Harish Mitter.

One day during this season of discontent she sends down word at Harish's arrival that she is too unwell to admit him. Harish weaves his way out into the dirty street below, clutching his hair, his eyes staring wide. Around him people make way for him as he wanders toward his car, thinking he's a madman or a drunk. He's a lover in pain. But in this neighborhood that's unlikely if not risible. Half his shirt hangs out of his belt and his silk jacket has a rip at the

shoulder from him trying to force his way past the stolid doorman who's seen and handled worse. Even standing patrons must be admitted or not only by order. Harish doesn't come for a week after that. Rehana cries herself maudlin. Pyari Bai scolds Rehana to bits.

Rehana cries muffling her face in her loverless bed. Pyari Bai says, "*Oyay!* You listen! Your father didn't marry me either! Hell, he didn't even bring me jewels and perfumes and English-style shoes to wear around the house like Mitter Sahib does."

"Do you even know who my father is?" Rehana screams, then shuts her door for hours.

Outside, Pyari Bai stands, her words died out, her ruined face and incongruously kohled eyes pincered by pain. She tells herself: this is the custom; this is how it is. You know that. You raise a child with the wages of your sin, and then they curse you for the life and fate you have given them. After a while she hobbles away on the arthritic hips of an old dancer.

After that week, though, Harish returns and of course Rehana relents. He tries to please her in other ways. He makes arrangements for her to do a voice-recording of one of her best-rendered *thumris*, and brings her a genuine gold-plated disc of the extended playing record. Pyari Bai's eyes shine with pride as well as greed. A few more of Rehana's songs are released commercially. She also receives more invitations to sing at weddings and follies of Bengali Babus, but Harish asks her not to accept these, and she obeys, still riding a fantastic flowered swing in the cooling breeze of the marriage fairytale universe.

There are men in her drawing room every night far more handsome, just as young, and at least rich enough. Somehow, though, it's Harish she wants to see, waits for. She has fallen in love, it would seem. Pyari Bai scolds her daughter again. "It's the Baiji's biggest mistake: to need the man instead of making sure that he needs and wants only her. Why only a courtesan's mistake, it's the mistake of any woman. Never let a man feel like he can have power if he wants it. Always keep him in beggar mode. The minute you let him think he has power over you, he puts one foot out the door."

But the dream remains, obdurate. And maybe it's the dream that makes it happen, since dreams can be stuffed into the heart through the gashes made by doomed loving. The wound, some poet says, is where the light comes in. And the dream grows into faith, into axiom, into poetry even. Six months into her fledgling modern career of gramophone singing, Rehana discovers she is pregnant. At first she can't be sure, but when the decrepit *Hakim* all the Baijis swear by pronounces her definitely with child, her heart fills with wayward hope.

When she tells Harish his face blazes first, then collapses. She clings to his arm, looking hopefully up into his face. He says very little more that evening, but holds her tighter to himself that night than he ever has. Her heart sinks. But he returns as expected the next evening and seems to be in fairly good spirits. She sings especially sweetly that night, feeling unfamiliar joy despite the uncertainty of the future. From behind the velvety curtains where she usually lolls, smoking her hookah while a maid presses swollen feet peeping out under voluminous ghaghra folds, Pyari Bai watches her daughter with anxious

scrutiny and dread. Mixed, as always, with a love so sharp it slices her heart.

Like in the bioscope, there's a great storm that night. Wind slaps the tops of tall trees and palms, sounding like a million hands beating breasts, moaning. Lightning spears darkness; thunder crackles so loud that Pyari Bai sends her reluctant apologies—"*gustakhi maaf*"—to Rehana's admirers, asking them to adjourn and depart for their residences in their assorted Bentleys, Aston Martins, Rolls Royces, Jeeps and even humbler Fiats and motorcycles. They all leave, expressing regret. Rehana was singing so exceptionally well tonight. To no one's surprise, Harish stays back.

The morning after, like the venerable trees and proud palms uprooted and tossed among flotsam and jetsam and an occasional broken animal carcass nauseating the drenched, cowering city, Rehana's hopes and dreams of being married lie blasted and withered.

"It's because I'm Muslim, isn't it? Suchitra's man took her—a nice Hindu man—and she's a Hindu. You Hindus hate us Muslims from the bottoms of your hearts, don't you?"

Harish winces. "Jaan, no Jaan! You know I love you! You know that the whole world could be against you and I'd still love you! You know that, Jaanu. You know I don't and shall never love another!"

"You love me but you can't marry me? How low a creature are you? You can't acknowledge this child? You don't have the courage for that? Who's ever heard of a real lover who doesn't have courage? Did Majnoon have courage for his Laila? Heer for Ranjha? Did Romeo die for Juliet?"

"Don't talk about dying, please, my best beloved," Harish begs. "We are so happy as things are! We can still be so happy! Of course I'll own our child as mine. Of course I'll take care of him and you forever! But how can my parents accept this? They can't. They'll never accept such a marriage. I may be able to persuade them to—"

"Oh ho ho, ai hai hai!" Rehana shrieks. Centuries-old kotha dirge oozes out in the twisted, warped syllables of a beautiful young mouth disfigured by pain. The whole kotha hears, jerked awake. It's another dawn of heartbreak. All the aunties know what it is, at once. Pyari Bai strikes her head with her palm and then keeps pounding it with her fist, pummeling in turns her pillow and her face. Writhing like a woman in childbirth.

"Big lover has come here, hai hai! He can love and he can fuck, but he can't marry! Oh, he can make babies but he can't tell his big daddy what he's done!" Harish clutches his head, covers his ears. Moans, totters out of bed, rushes to the window, pushes his head out, shaking it as if to dislodge the sounds of wounded rage.

"What did I ever do to you but love you?" Rehana howls. "What did I ever do to you? Why are you doing this to me?"

Then. "Did you ever love me?????"

Harish will never forget the crescendo of that question. For years, for the rest of his life, the sounds will crash again and again on the borders of his mind, sleeping, dreaming, or waking. He will wonder where she went. Where she took the child.

From the brothel section of Bowbazar, where the kotha is, it's about twenty minutes by rickshaw and a few by taxi to Bow Barracks. Bow Barracks is an old cantonment area where the sweepings of empire have gathered as Anglo-Indians and Christians, where a certain puttering, angled mode of English is punctuated by "*babaa*" and "*come naa*," and so on. In one particular house there, like many others painted red with green shutters, Pyari Bai and Rehana and a single maid put up after the move from the Bowbazar Kotha. Rehana has her baby there.

Then she becomes Jolene.

She does this with the help of Anglo-India and Christian girls of the neighborhood who take charge, knowing her history, one that many of their mothers, and some of them, have lived. Through some of it Rehana is barely aware of her surroundings, of those around her. Only when her son wails she shakes loose a torpor that otherwise mercifully cradles her in its close embrace.

Her hair is bobbed and dyed a bluish black, her eyebrows plucked and penciled into thin arches, *angrakhas*, and *salwar kameezes* exchanged for low-cut frocks and patent leather pumps. When the whole transformation is finished— complete with an education in basic spoken English—Jolene sits back and regards the thing she has created. It has taken almost a year. Then she weeps.

Yes, she's very sentimental that way. She's always loved bioscope music of the sort she'd begun making herself. Far more, in fact, than the kind of *tawaifi* singing that she had to master for a livelihood. She would have liked to sing for the bioscope, but all that's gone.

Then one day like any other Jolene sallies forth into a new world of clubs, dancing, and partying late with officers of the many armies crawling all over British Calcutta. She forsakes the protected dewiness of her past self for something tougher, powdered, and lacquered. The baby stays home with Pyari Bai and gurgles when he sees his mother, but she hardly ever picks him up. If someday she has to give him up for good, it's better this way.

Herself, she will be someone's wife some day and set up house, for real. Naturally, like other lovely women who stoop to one or other kind of folly with men who betray, she imagines love forever massacred in her heart. But a husband, home, and respectability she will have.

Harish glimpses her just once during his increasingly frequent and erratic nocturnes, but what with being blotto and also half-witless in grief most of the time, he doesn't recognize her as once upon a time Rehana. The transformation is an entire success.

CHAPTER 51

It's grim out there. Roma knows. She understands. There's a big war going on. Sometimes she wonders if Roderick is out there fighting. Maybe he decided not to be a sailor. It's been a long time since he's been heard from. If

he does send letters, the whole household doesn't get to hear of them as was once the case.

Inside her too there's grimness. Darkness. She doesn't know what will become of her. When Mashimoni dies, who will take care of her? How will she stay on in the house? Won't Harish marry, have a family? Will Harish's wife let her stay? What's it like to be the poor, spinster aunt, and not even a blood relation?

As usual, she storms Prem with her recurrent complaints about life, and the theme of the bioscope. "Mashimoni, Harish knows so many people in the bioscope industry," she grumbles. "He can easily take me to a producer or director for an audition. It's not beyond him. He just doesn't try. No one in this house cares when it comes to me." Prem is so fed up with the whining—her own thoughts wander now in another world and a time she'd been sure she'd rubbed out forever, beyond restoration, and she resorts to a black pellet oftener than she wants to—that she asks Harish to please, please take the befuddled young woman to someone, somewhere, to try to see if she can get a role, any role, in some production, any production, except anything vulgar.

"Didi isn't exactly . . . you know Mother, what I'm saying"—Prem sadly nods at this—"and besides the bioscope world is not in great shape either right now. Raw stock is in extremely short supply; studios are shutting down. It's not that easy to make films these days, or to get someone into films. . . ."

In the end, though, he decides to try Pandey-ji, the one film industry persona he respects and likes, with whom Roma will at least be safe if not successful. Casting couch stories are plentiful, and they're surely not all baseless. He tries not to think of Rehana, for whom once he didn't perform such an errand for selfish reasons.

Roma is beyond excited. The day of her visit—a euphemism for the crass word "audition"—she dresses herself to the gills, georgette and glitter from head to toe, the pages of glamor magazines her main inspiration, but also society figures. She has decorated her buxom mignon of raven hair with jasmines. A little outlandish, or perhaps it's artistic; hard to say for sure. She's wearing a daring outfit—a silver-brocaded, translucent black georgette sari that falls about her feet in soft folds and layers, a somewhat brief white satin blouse with full see-through chiffon sleeves cuffed at the wrist, and a cape of diaphanous shot silk gathered at her throat with a diamond flower pin lent to her for the occasion by a dubious but silent Prem. She can either trail the cape behind her or gather it about her petite form, whichever the director prefers. When finished, the mirror reflects back her sartorial skill.

Roma has learned to dress well. It's an adventurous time in spite of or maybe because of the war. She envies and vies with, in spirit if not in substance, that *belle de jour*, that social butterfly par excellence, Lady Edwina Mountbatten, India's last British viceroy's wife, who's rumored to be having a torrid affair with the princeling of Congress, Gandhi-ji's right hand and ear, Pundit Jawaharlal Nehru, another Inner Temple lawyer like Gandhi himself. In spirit, Roma knows she's the equal of any female Don Juan. Her resources being somewhat limited, she reinvents herself every day with adventuress styles and

outfits, little flourishes and frissons that pay tribute to her daring and stylishness, beauty itself be hanged for there's enough of that going around and no one much the happier for it, are they? Look at Mashimoni herself, she thinks.

Pandey-ji has been in the business a long time. Of course he's his eternal gracious, kindly self, but Harish catches at once the regretful incredulity in his gaze seeing Roma.

"What kinds of films do you like, Miss Chatterjee?"

Roma names many. She tells Pandey-ji in a hopeful effusion that she began thinking of the bioscope and acting when she went to see *Nala Damayanti* with her Mashimoni, Harish's mother. She tells him, fawningly, that she idolizes him, always has. Pandey-ji doesn't cease smiling but he looks down at the floor in unpropitious embarrassment. Then he explains to Roma that he wants to usher in a new Golden Age of Bengali Cinema. Create a legacy and remind Bengalis of their own creativity, their heritage, their genius. He speaks as he looks away or down, though, and again Harish's heart sinks. And aches for Roma.

Roma gives her audition.

"A bioscope that will make Bengalis respect—no, worship—women again, and believe in family, love and sincerity. That's my hope and my dream." Those are Pandey-ji's kindly words as Roma and Harish leave. He will review her screen test as soon as pressing business allows him some time. He looks mildly, benignly at Roma and his glasses twinkle.

Roma doesn't know what he's talking about, clearly. She looks anxious. But a shadow comes and goes in her eyes.

"Because for too long we've had tired melodrama, nauseating tear-jerkers and tawdry tragedies. Haven't we?"

Roma nods, uncertain.

Pandey-ji certainly has the gift of the gab. Harish understands that he will let Roma down gently, very gently. He also understands why he's been a great success in the cut-throat, desperado film industry. His poetry is the moving image, and he its keening bard.

Indeed, in a few days Jagat Pandey tells Harish: "She doesn't have any real talent to speak of, my friend. The plainness I could work with, even give her good character roles. But she can't act! I can't do anything with that."

Seeing the look on Harish's face he relents. "I could maybe cast her in a bit part like—you know—sister-in-law, or neighborhood friend. Maybe a nurse or a housekeeper. Yes, that might be possible. She wouldn't have many lines."

Harish thanks him and leaves. Pandey-ji says, "Do let me know."

"What did he say?" Roma meets Harish at the front entrance as soon as he comes home. One look at him tells her that he hasn't exactly come to crown her the new queen of the Golden Age of Bengali Bioscope.

"Didi, yes he said he might have something, but let me come in and cool off, please."

Roma's face falls but she waits with an ill grace. Harish flees to his bedroom and doesn't come down till dinner time, an hour or so later. Roma hasn't been pounding the foyer or anything but as soon as dinner is over she looks at Harish and makes a very slight movement of her head but one that will clearly

brook no further waiting. Resigned, Harish leads the way to the informal sitting room, Roma at his heels.

"He could offer you a role as a supporting character."

"What kind of supporting character?"

"Well, someone close to the female lead . . ."

"I suppose that might do to start with," Roma says. "After all, I have no experience. Did he say when I can start?"

"Well, he said he'll let us know . . ."

"What does that mean? Didn't he say he was starting a new movie, something about a Golden Age?"

"That was about a new *kind* of movie, a better *kind* than the dreadful trash being made these days."

"Okay, okay, I don't need to know all that," Roma renews sharply. "Just tell me what kind of supporting role?"

Harish says he has no specific information yet. He has more presence of mind than to mention bit parts: a loose-lipped neighborhood shrew, a sprightly maidservant, a housekeeper. And he feels tremendously sorry for Roma. He sees that she feels that her springtime has come and maybe is about to leave.

He doesn't bring up the subject with Pandey-ji again and Pandey-ji, with innate good sense and compassion, doesn't revert to it either.

Roma goes into a wintry despair. Especially, she refuses to go to the bioscope anymore, for so long her favorite recreation. When Prem invites her she says she has a headache; the movie will be of no interest to her; she's tired. Anything and everything. And she doesn't work on a believability that she knows is not expected. Harish knows she's truly crushed when she doesn't bring up the question of the audition again with him.

Why has she always set her heart on what's thought to be beyond her reach? Dominance. Roderick. Being an actress. She wouldn't know if asked, wouldn't recognize the condition as her own. She doesn't know that she wants to be special; all she knows is that she simply wants her due. The world owes her much. The world owes her something.

But the world is at war, an epic of hatred, rage and suffering. People won't remember it much except those who must, whose lives—as they knew them—are blown apart. Villages torn off the face of the earth. Women raped, then beheaded. Children bayoneted and crushed by rolling tanks as they lie dying. People will later think of the Second World War (again) as "the war to end all wars"—but now all the news is of POW camps. Only the lucky return, stick figures, hollow-eyed, from the edge of the abyss.

1942. Burma is in danger of falling to the Japanese. The Japanese are marching, snarling at India's borders. Sir Mitter talks about the pragmatic Americans and of pragmatism as the reality of life.

Then bombs fall in Pearl Harbor. America joins the war. Sir Naren is stumped and then even more effusive in praise of that great country. "By Jove,

what a great country!" he takes to saying. He says it like a child holding a splen-
did, live fire-cracker in his hands, usually in the company of other stalwart men.

In August 1942 a young Royal Air Force Sergeant visits Mitter Mansion.

Without notice, without announcement, he shows up that sweltering August day. Hard to trace in him the thin boy who was always outgrowing his
clothes once. When someone announces Sergeant Hartfield requesting leave
to see Lady Mitter, Prem is reading the paper. Her Lady Mitter and Prem
parts are especially not talking these days. The world looks very bleak to her.
There is no way back to the past, not even to atone for all the mistakes. The
past and all its loves and suffering are history. The children she's been spared
are unhappy: neither Harish nor Roma seems to have a bright day. Sir Naren
is sinking deeper each day into the quicksand of not knowing to whom the
next half century belongs, though he's very sure it won't be Indians ruling
India. Duffers and peons, he says; how can they? She sometimes wonders what
he will do if India does gain independence. In the thick of 1942's great Quit
India movement Sir Naren clings to the idea that his lifelong overlords will
not only beat the Germans and the Japanese at their game, but also the likes
of Gandhi and Subhash Bose.

When the name Hartfield is pronounced it's like a live wire held to Prem's
tired heart. One part of her travels back to that morning in 1916 when she
first heard the name Hartfield. Lilian came, and Roderick came with her. Losing Roderick scrapes the point of a rusty nail across her heart; it always will.
And now a Sergeant Hartfield is here. Wants to see her. In a few seconds she
untangles the name Hartfield and the Sergeant part from one another. Her lips
tremble while her heart is wrung by joy and fear at once. Roderick? He never
wrote to say he was coming. She feels like throwing her arms around blind
chance and dancing with it.

A few moments later, blinded by tears that didn't brook decent pause or
permission, she's saying: "Roderick! Is it really you, Roderick? Oh my boy, my
boy!

"T!"

Roderick helps her down to a chair. She's been taking a few too many of
the pellets lately, and she promises herself, in her joy, to stop now.

His face is harder but still boyish.

He's come back. His uniform's ridges dent her face. She doesn't mind.
"Roderick."

"T, how have you been? How are you? My dear, dear T!"

Prem sits smiling unguardedly, clutching Roderick, for the next two or
three hours as the rest of the household comes to see him, to exclaim over him,
to touch him, to gawk, to rush up and hug him as if they were stealth bombers.
Like some naïve, unselfconscious woman from a village many lifetimes ago—
some woman who must have made her possible, maybe the foremother who
saved the gold anklets for her—Prem grins broadly, dreamily saying to people:

"Look . . . our Roderick. He's come back."

Harish comes and grasps Roderick's hand. He can't speak. Roderick folds him in a bear hug.

Roma comes.

Roderick bops her on the head. "What? Still unmarried?" She's already rushed up and glued herself to him. Her eyes are shut tight with all the weight of her bliss.

No one chides him, not even fondly. Everyone forgives him for having been gone. Everyone sees that with him, a new time has come. Everyone forgives him everything.

Roderick was posted in Burma. He only has a few days of furlough now, but soon he will be moved to Calcutta. He will come to Alipore every one of those days, he vows. Men on the fields are dying like flies, he also says. Best make the best use of time, he grins. He and his fellow RAF officers mainly fly supply and aid missions. Night and day, cloud and sun and rain, fresh or near-dead, as long as they can sit up in the cockpit and see, they fly supplies and weapons across the "Hump."

That's what they call the northern Himalayas. Mostly Allied American and British Air Force pilots have been performing incredible feats of flight over them, bringing supplies to beleaguered China from the India-Burma border. Over eight hundred airmen will die in these flights, but between 1942–1945 many thousands of planes fly the "Hump"—scraggy five-mile-high Himalayan mountain ranges—and bring indispensable wartime supplies to the Chinese army cut off by the Japanese occupation of Thailand, Burma, and Malaysia. The "Hump" pilots brave the dreaded Japanese Air Force. The feats of these pilots of the "forgotten army" of the China-Burma-India theater of war will later inspire and educate American, British, Canadian, Australian, French, New Zealander, and South African pilots of the Berlin Airlifts (1948–49) who will fly in supplies to a beleaguered west Berlin blockaded by an increasingly combative cold war-era Soviet Union. But also, whenever they can they bring down the Japanese Sally bombers that buzz at the borders of Calcutta.

The people of Calcutta love their city. It's their entire geography of motherland. Defending Calcutta is defending civilization. Unabashedly partisan and salt of the earth, all Calcutta will soon love Roderick.

Roderick never says it himself, but Harish pieces together that he's downed more Japanese Sallys than any other officer in the eastern command. For one, he often flies supply missions over Burmese forests where American and British soldiers are hiding and fighting Japs. Some place called Nhpum Ga, for instance, he says. He's flown over that one often, and recently. Harish feels stunned, awed, irrationally exuberant despite the constant ache in his heart.

Roderick says he has specifically requested to be transferred to the air defense of Calcutta. He wants to fly the most dangerous missions. Normally superior officers don't allow such a young pilot to undertake many flight shifts in quick succession. It's not standard practice. But RAF Sergeant Hartfield is counting on his fervent rhetoric to overcome all objections, ferret out every loophole for permission.

Sir Naren surreptitiously wipes his eyes and determines to pull every possible string to block such orders. His son, just returned, mustn't be up in the thundering skies where no one's a god, and there's no God. Sir Naren is an atheist himself but suddenly he feels weak enough to remember the word.

The week after, everyone is, as always, invited to Lady Sinha's annual garden party. It's always a grand affair ending in dusk to dawn drunken joy and concupiscence for some, and righteous indignation and self-congratulation for those others who leave early. In other words, it's always good fun. At the party there are many beauties with pleasing curves wrapped in glossy, gossamer saris or sparkling frocks; beribboned, be-ringed, gem-fire flashing from their delicate earlobes and slender necks; their dainty feet encased in daintier shoes. Coveted, young, highbred, they move like gazelles—a few bolder ones like lithe, rearing Arabs. Notwithstanding this, this night Roma is resolved to have as many dances with Roderick as possible.

This new occasion sits slightly lopsided with their memories of childhood play and pranks. But she and Roderick dance with each other so much that Lady Sinha, naturally nosy, raises one pencil-thin eyebrow. The little group she's queening over all look at the dancers. And so a pince-nez or two also goes up here and there.

During a brief pause in the music Roderick and Roma sit down, panting.

"Fancy that," Roderick says. He's grinning from ear to ear.

Roma clasps his arm and lays her head on his shoulder. "How much fun this is, isn't it?"

Roderick nods, absent-minded, looking around.

"Roderick! I'm talking to you!" Roma pouts.

"Yes, Mademoiselle, I'm all attention."

"I want not just attention! I want you to be all mine!"

"What? All yours? With all these beauties prancing around? Can't I dance with even a few of them?"

"Roderick, I'm serious. I'm going to have you all to myself, you just see."

"And how will that be done, dear Mademoiselle?" Roderick lights a cigarette and offers Roma one. She would take it but she's afraid of Lady Sinha's eyebrow and also she doesn't think it would suit her as well as the young women with long, pale, delicate arms and fancy cigarette holders. She'll probably look like an earthy beedi-smoking type. She shakes her head.

"By making you marry me, as you promised you would."

"I did?"

At this Roma rises in a huff and walks away, and after a few more puffs of the cigarette Roderick tosses it into a half-drunk gin and tonic nearby and goes in search of her. He doesn't find her, and so he dances with a few other young lovelies who are tremulous to be dancing with this young, dashing officer who's already made a splash and a big name as Calcutta's "knight-errant."

Simpering, one says, "You should be careful Captain Hartfield! We read about all your dare-devil deeds."

Courteous as ever he replies, "Only Sergeant, Miss . . ."

The simperer hastily says, "Roy . . . Miss Roy . . ."

"Ah yes, I beg your pardon, Miss Roy. That's what I do, though. It's what I did when I flew the Hump. That's what I'll be doing in Calcutta."

"We can't thank you enough of course," Miss Roy hastens to say, "but we wish you wouldn't take such terrible risks."

Smiling a mischievously polite smile Roderick says, "You are too kind, Miss Roy. I shall remember that."

Roma looks at herself in a bathroom mirror and frowns. She has a little lipstick smudged around the corner of her mouth and her face powder is patchy. It's such a hot afternoon, who throws a garden party in such heat, Roma grouses silently. She fixes her slip ups, makes a moue at the mirror, and sallies forth, trying to pick up her courage along the way to play the role of the confident frontrunner that she intends to be.

"Ah, there you are!" Roderick says on spotting her. He comes to her with his long arms wide open. Roma can't stay angry. They go back to the dancing at once. At one point during the next bout of dancing her sari's long cascading end falling from a brooch pinned to her shoulder wraps itself around Roderick's trouser legs. It's the closest thing to an erotic embrace she's ever had.

Such happiness. But is it possible to be so happy? How is it possible to be so happy? Roma thinks.

Lines from some poet she read in school come to her: the desire of the moth for the star.

In the Rolls Royce on the way back Roma expects to be soundly scolded by Prem, and indeed gets a little fussing, but beyond that there's something else in Mashimoni's eyes. As if she's just seen something for the first time. She looks very happy after a very long time. Her hand with its heavy diamond ring lies between them on the seat of the Rolls; to her surprise Roma sees her fingers tap as if the music is still playing.

Roderick lives in army quarters in Barrackpore. This is where the allied British soldiers in Calcutta live for the most part. It is swampy, mosquito infested, noisy, primitively supplied, and far from the flash parts of the city like Park Street, the Parade grounds, the Strand, Chowringhee, and Alipore. And from Mitter Mansion. These soldiers will become the Forgotten Army of the China Burma India (CBI) theatre of war even before the war is over. Somehow, what happens in Asia never makes the big news in the annals of world history. The war offices in London and Washington, DC already don't pay these soldiers much mind; they think they have much bigger worries elsewhere.

In some sense the Barrackpore quarters, far and roughshod as they are, are safer for Roderick. This is how Prem and Sir Naren—separately—console themselves for Roderick's billeting. Englishmen, or even Kutcha Bachchas, are more and more often becoming targets of mob rage. The Congress and Gandhi-ji want the British to promise to 'Quit India,' and Churchill thunders at the opportune cunning and self-involvement of Indians. Don't they know there's a war going on?

The Indians say, "Oh yes, we know there's a war going on." This is exactly why we want a promise, now, while the war's going on, and loyal Indians are fighting for the Commonwealth and the King, that the British will leave after

the war. The British say, "Nothing doing; just wait!" Even Gandhi-ji is fasting less. The muscle and blood rather than the gastric hollows of India are building momentum. At this point city streets are not always safe for white men.

But from his quarters, Roderick comes most afternoons in his roaring Jeep, like a handsome Bedouin riding out of a dust storm.

Part 7:
Dulce est, decorum est, pro patria mori; Calcutta, 1942–

CHAPTER 52

Like every year, the Mitters throw their annual ball. Lady Mitter's parties and dinners are popular events. Everybody who's anybody comes to them, and the guest list is highly select. Afterwards people talk for weeks, of course, about the décor, the food, the drinks, the fashions, the debutantes, the music, the dancing. Until the next year, when they are ready to be dazzled all over again.

The night of this party in 1942, Prem stands as customary at the foot of the great stairs in the hallway, greeting guests. She appears queen of all she sees. People may be forgiven for thinking this. People can hardly be expected to know that a desire to vanish lurks in her heart every day, growing a little stronger each day. She has been standing and greeting the world for a long time. That's Lady Mitter's job.

As she smiles, she wonders: Could there have been another life? Another family? Another man? Could she have been that man's wife? She dreams again of the village these days. She dreams of Jagat Pandey. She remembers how thin he was, how frayed his clothes were. How battered his shoes were. All those letters. Never given to her. He never got any replies. Where is he now? Dead? Since the night she found the letters, somehow she thinks he can't be dead. It's a fanciful idea, she knows.

But. This is her real life. Her family. This house. Her creation. She has made all this happen. Of course she is the queen of all she surveys. From mere money, and most of it dirty—she knows this for a fact—she's brought style and beauty into this house. From chaos and suffering she's created a family. Motley, maybe, but happier than the alternative. And now even Roderick is back.

The guests look at her admiringly. She's dressed for adoration. Her still jet-black hair is done in a grand mignon. Mignons are back in fashion these days. Diamonds glitter in it, catching the brilliance of the thousand-piece Bohemian chandelier. She's wearing a deep-blue and silver brocade silk. Her sari covers a silver-beaded satin blouson shirt waist that emphasizes that erect and still slender carriage. She's still a handsome woman.

The letters are in the trunk. The trunk is now in her vast wardrobe. Nothing in it has been removed. She will never open it again. The vial of pellets is under her couch, still almost half-full. There is no portrait of her mother in the house, and she will never again touch the one in the trunk: Saroj Devi Aulakh and Akshaya Aulakh will never be parted again.

But today Harish is already here, and Roma, and Sir Naren is around somewhere, held together with tuxedo, bow tie, pince-nez, pipe, and self-satisfaction. Roderick is coming. This is her life. Not a bad life in the end. She has found love and loved in unlikely places again and again.

Everyone is waiting tonight for Roderick, the uncrowned prince of

fairytales in wartime Calcutta. Since Lady Sinha's party, he's flown a record number of times more and chased the Japanese away from Calcutta many times. Prem smiles, momentarily imagining the things people will begin to say when he arrives. A ripple will pass through the room. The swashbuckling Roderick Hartfield himself! Sergeant Hartfield, the legendary slayer of the Japanese bombers incongruously called 'Sally'! 'Knight beaufighter!' Such grand names they've given him. Each one more than well deserved.

Most everyone else of consequence has been announced, greeted and discreetly crossed off the guest list by the professional staff hired for the party. Prem decides to give herself a short reprieve in her private parlor—she's been trying to be very good of late, cutting the pellets into quarters or smaller if at all—until Roderick arrives. Walking past Sir Naren where he stands with a group of his cronies, she hears the conversation and a few stray words. They slow down her steps.

"They don't think or feel like us. Why should the best of society be encumbered by the riffraff, the inferior types and their endless bad tendencies?"

This is the Honorable Mr. Lister, one of the eminent medical men of Calcutta who's just been recognized and distinguished by the Crown. A little knot of pear-shaped grandees is standing around him, some with pipes in their mouths, listening and nodding.

Then Sir Naren speaks. "Indeed! Doubtless! Lives not worth living, I say. As a member of the Aryan race myself I do completely see the worthiness of that approach to our many social problems."

"After all, the Jews have brought it on themselves," another grandee offers.

Though she should sail on past, Prem can't move. Before her eyes once again is the thin body of Jagat Pandey, in frayed clothes and battered shoes. Again, he's eating his lunch of dry rotis, pickle, and a bit of onion or hot chili under a solitary tree, with the sun burning the surrounding grass ochre. She shouldn't say a word but she can't hold it back. She walks up to the gentlemen. Seeing the lady of the house approach, they make vaguely appreciative sounds.

"Are you saying, Sir Naren, that those who come from different classes and fortunes should be eliminated? That the poor are unworthy of living? Or the races are never to mingle? Are you of the party of our modern Satan, Hitler himself?"

She has spoken more ringingly than she'd realized. The sudden silence can be cut with a knife.

Sir Naren partially unfreezes, frowns horribly, and says in his best blaw blaw, "I'm saying, my lady, that certain experiments and actions already in progress in western civilization, to properly classify and rein in the sort of people who reproduce endlessly and cannot feed the mouths they bring into this world, do demonstrate the advantages of distinguishing peons from princes."

In the deep silence Prem and Sir Naren's eyes lock. It's a dare. He knows what she's thinking, and she knows he knows it.

"Certain experiments?"

Everyone knows, really, who Roderick's father is. She has always protected both father and son. Her behavior this evening is quite shocking and she knows

it. He knows that she knows it. Still, he is the first to look away.

"And so Hitler is doing the world a favor, Sir Naren?"

A gracious aristocratic hostess doesn't speak like this at a party, least of all at her own. As if she's itching for a fight with her worthy husband. Some people are already wide-eyed, ears cocked for more. But Prem reads newspapers, more than even her husband. Sometimes, after reading a particular report of war losses or news from Germany, she takes a little black pellet to numb herself. But this evening she's absolutely, starkly clearheaded. She hasn't taken one since Roderick's return because she's happy after a long time. On the other hand, Jagat comes in her dreams a lot more since Roderick returned. Dead or alive, he comes. Well, he'd said, "Forever."

The knot of gentlemen loosens, spreads out a little, but lingers, watches. Mouths clamped over pipes and cheroots, paws cupping crystal goblets of cognac and other ambrosia.

Prem finds herself trembling. Someone puts their arm around her. It's Harish. He speaks to her gently, softly, but loud enough that people nearby can hear. "Come Mother, let me get you a glass of champagne. The belle of the ball shouldn't be standing with her hands empty, right everyone?" Some cheer, and the wall of silence crashes down. Silently Prem squeezes her son's hand. How blessed she is in her children at least. This is a thing she must try never to forget. She forces up a smile and walks away with Harish. She can feel the many eyes on her back. She's not sorry for what she just did. Somehow, she feels, she's paid tribute to a poor soldier who loved her, and died not knowing that she didn't get any of his letters.

No sign of Roderick yet. It is eight o'clock in the evening and the last light is fading outside. The lambent greenery wrapping Alipore like a soft Kashmir shawl is darkening quickly into a stony jade. Christmas is only a few weeks away. All over central Calcutta, especially around the military airspaces near Chowringhee and Park Street, lights blaze or twinkle all night. White and black men play jazz into the dark eastern night; sometimes a raucous, strapping woman belts out songs about being blue and in love at Trinca's or Firpo's or at the Ming Room. Customers stagger in and out, GIs and British boys sometimes arm in arm, sometimes ready to cut each other's throat. The immense Christmas tree at Whiteway and Laidlaw's soothes many a young white boy still wet behind the ears who has left his heart behind in Texas or Montana or Yorkshire. Though Christmas is almost three weeks away, the slight wintry chill that Calcutta experiences in December has set in—the air is bright and crisp.

But what is that?

Suddenly noise as though from another end of the city ripples past and around the house. People rush to the large windows to look up and see, unmistakably, that a silent flotilla of aircraft has darkened the sky. The band has stopped and there's shouting in the street. "*Japanee! Japanee! Japanee* coming!" Harish huffs and puffs across the hallway to find the household gathered around

the great dining table, someone tuning in vain the radiogram that should have been playing carols and military marches but now fills the room with static interrupted by pops, shrieks, and whistles. The Japanese, despite Chevalier Hartfield's valor and courage, have unimaginably come back to bomb Calcutta, weeks before Christmas. Can this really happen? Of course it can. That's why Roderick is not here.

News comes that the Japs have targeted Howrah Bridge and then raked the Kidderpore docks. Sir Naren loudly, inarticulately curses the Japanese, and Subhash Bose who's turned traitor to his own country and joined the Axis powers. Even Gandhi isn't as great a scoundrel as Bose. Let them all go to hell! Prem looks at the pale faces around her and draws herself up in spite of her terrible dread and panic.

It's her duty to rally the weak and fearful, both as an Indian and as Lady Mitter. More drinks are served, though the band is not inclined to start up again.

Once the raid seems over—no shrieks, rattle, and whistles for an hour or so—the guests leave, go home, go to the clubs, go to the barracks, to the airfields. One by one the house lights that had been switched off hastily and too late in any case, come back on.

Newspapers the next morning report Flight Sergeant Hartfield missing in action. The army looks for him for five days but his body is not found, though his copilot is found in the swamps in the eastern part of the city, stuck in brambles in the jungles off the Hooghly. The copilot's face is unrecognizable. Burnt severely. Looks as though he tried to get away after the crash.

Life goes on. For about a month, little boys will cry for the fallen hero; still, life goes on. The newspapers scream abuse at the Royal Air Force, especially the Alipore Squadron 67; in return civilian grumbling gets soundly thwacked by RAF planes flying dangerously low over the weekend Alipore horse race. A few more bombs fall over Calcutta like burning leaves in a mournful autumn. The children of Bengal—a faithless, spineless Bengal according to the British, ready to turn from the Raj to adoring Subhash Bose amidst rumors of his rising Indian National Army at the drop of a sign from the sky!—still chant during their war games:

Sa re ga ma pa dha ni
Bom felechhe japanni
Bomer bhetor keutey shaap
British bole baap re baap

Do re me fa so la ti
Bombs come from Japan almighty
The cobra springs out of the bomb
The British lose all their aplomb

But life is definitely on pause in Mitter Mansion. Roma doesn't believe the newspapers. Roderick can't be dead. What an idea! And, for herself, if one dream didn't come true—the dream of being an actress—surely the other

dream of someday marrying Roderick can't vanish too! This is not a tragic melodrama movie. People don't know how to wait, she keeps telling herself and anyone else who will listen. Roderick will return. She knows it. Maybe right now he's making his way back here. Wounded, maybe, but very much alive. How the whole city can so quickly lose faith in the man they call a hero, she can't understand.

"I don't understand, Mashimoni, why everyone's giving up so quickly. After all, nobody has been found! Why can't people just keep quiet and wait a little longer? This is very annoying!" She blusters to Prem.

CHAPTER 53

It's the sixth day after the crash. Prem looks like a much older woman. Her hair is uncombed and pulled back in an uncharacteristic haphazard bun, loose, untidy strands falling into her eyes and standing up around her head like a faint gray halo. There are deep, dark circles under her eyes, and her skin looks dry and bleached. Sir Naren hasn't even come to dinner since the day the news came. The meals are a funereal affair with Roma, Harish, and Prem sitting at three ends of the table, the seat Roderick usually took empty, again, as well as Sir Naren's seat at the head of the table. Even then Roma frets and gibbers along the same lines, alternating between cheering and scolding the other two.

As follows, one afternoon: "Oh come on now, one would think the end of the world had come from looking at you! Roderick will come back! I'm sure of it. He's an excellent pilot. Excellent!"

Prem's head has been hanging between her shoulders, her face looking down at her knees. Her face is puffy, eyes almost closed. She looks at Roma now. It's just the two of them. Teatime on the sixth day. The tea in the cups has grown cold and filmy. Prem's eyes are dull and glazed, yet full of something Roma will not look at, will not acknowledge. "Mashimoni, buck up!" Roma goes on. "People don't just disappear like that, you know! Roderick is too good a pilot, too clever for that." Prem attempts a nod, doesn't finish it, then gets up and shuffles out of the room.

On the eighth day of the search for Flight Sergeant Hartfield the Army declares it a lost cause and ends the search.

Again, Roma professes derision at this news as well. As the radio announcer drones on about the great tragedy, the terrible loss, the heroic spirit, the tremendous sacrifice etc., she swats the words away like bothersome flies. Roderick is coming back. And that's that. Roderick always does what he says he'll do. So he won't quit. Others might not return. Roderick will.

The clock ticks, the hours turn. And Roma begins to agonize. She abandons efforts to make the others board the dinghy of hope she's on. So she must find an ally, a resource elsewhere. In desperation she makes an appeal to the only person she can think of asking for more help.

Gyan Sengupta is kind to her for some reason. He normally keeps a low profile, and especially the last year or so he has seemed more secretive, more evasive than ever. His work is done meticulously, punctiliously as always, but he no longer seems much available to Sir Naren outside of that. No more long closed-door conferences in the library. He doesn't even come to the house much; says he prefers to keep his work at the office so as to not disturb the family.

"I'm very sorry, Miss Chatterjee," Sengupta repeats several times on the phone. But Roma doesn't want condolences. She needs him to understand that Roderick isn't dead. He can't be. The search for him has been dropped too soon. Will he please, please, use any contacts Sir Naren might have to see if the authorities can be made to recognize their error and resume their search. Doesn't Sir Naren know a lot of people at the newspapers? Surely people can write articles or letters to the editor that will convince the authorities that this search has been abandoned untimely. "Or, if that doesn't work," she says in a lower voice, "perhaps you know some people who may have more local connections, or information about things the police don't know?"

Humans are selfish, but someone else's pain sometimes opens the sluices of one's own grief. Sengupta has grief of his own. He's lost people dear to him too, especially lately, as the violent protests against British rule have grown. Also as Hindus and Muslims are regularly turning on each other, enraged by the separatist politics of the British and the desperate lunging away of the Muslim League from the idea of one India on the one hand, and what to many seem Gandhi-ji's puerile, idealistic platitudes on the other hand.

Sengupta works for Naren Mitter, of course, but there's a greater cause and a higher being he serves. As much as he has no regrets about the death of any English dog, the expression he imagines on Roma's face as she speaks imprints itself on him. It's the expression his mother had the day his father died in the famine that brought them to the city as refugees.

"Of course, Miss Chatterjee—I'll do all I can—yes, yes, no doubt that is true—no doubt further searching will . . . yes, please rest, good night good night. . . ."

A day later Roma calls him again at the office on Rawdon Street. "I'm sorry to bother you, but any news? The papers are not reporting anything."

He asks for another day, maybe two. "I'm sure there'll be some news . . . some good news, I'll see what . . ."

Roma doesn't call again. Rigor mortis begins spreading over hope.

Then she, too, crashes. She closes her mind and ears to people talking about the healing power of time, especially the maid who brings her food in her bed. She hardly knows who or what's around her. She's sure her heart will never mend. She asks herself what curse accompanies her that people die from it. She tells herself that she's lost her final chance at happiness. When she dreams at night, freeing herself with difficulty from the barbed wires of consolation, she hears her grandmother cursing her. She hears moaning. Who moans? For what? It's herself.

Sometimes Roderick floats into the darkness of the dream, reminding her that she killed her mother at birth. She wakes shuddering, babbling in the gray

February dawn, in the light of her new understanding that life does hold terrible mysteries revealed only in suffering, in the discovery that human beings are playthings of chance. She hardly eats, sleeps only in a state of fitful delirium, the tears already pooled in her eyes every time she wakes up.

Her mother also comes in her dreams. She doesn't know her mother's face very well; there is only one faded gray sepia photo that Mashimoni gave her years ago. In the dream she, Roma, married happily to a very nice man whose face is always blurry, takes her mother shopping, buys her nice things: rich saris, gold earrings, a handbag, maybe a Kashmir shawl. Because her mother usually otherwise can be found sitting half in sunlight and half in darkness at the door onto the terrace of an unknown house, fish scales and bones scattered about the dim, murky hallway seen through the door. She sits astride a vertical slicer with a wooden base, the *bonti* Indian women use instead of knives, always chopping, slicing, peeling, quartering, halving vegetables, meat, fish, anything and everything. There's also an awful smell around her; rats scamper about chasing cockroaches with massive antennae. But since Roma, her only daughter, so lucky, so well married, can afford to buy her many nice things, maybe she doesn't suffer so much any longer even if she has to cook, clean, and work so much.

Roma sees in the dream the winking of gold from the fashionable jewelry on her own wrists, her fingers, neck, ears. Though she's wearing the vermillion required of married Hindu women, her hair is cut in a fashionable modern bob, since the man with the blurry face likes it that way.

When Roma is awake, Prem comes shuffling, unsteady, to urge her to eat, to take a shower, change her clothes. Roma refuses, and Prem retreats. She too is so tired. She doesn't have the strength to carry another person on her back anymore. Sir Naren is now seriously ill, completely bedridden. The doctors can't really diagnose the trouble. Prem knows that it's his broken heart. She wishes she too could lie down and never get up again; her heart is so heavy it must be breaking too. But she can't. Because? Well, she can't. It's her duty to stay standing as long as she can.

She hasn't taken a pellet yet. Just in case Roderick comes back. She must be present, awake, alert. It takes great effort not to take out the vial, but she somehow manages. Sometimes she thinks of the hackneyed phrase, 'A hero's death.' Sometimes she wants to bomb the whole lexicon of honor and heroism out of existence.

CHAPTER 54

Yellow isn't a great color in this year, 1942. This is clear to Amherst Ishiru Buck, so-called American Hero of the 'Forgotten Army' of the Allies, in the war to end all wars.

Sergeant Buck does not want to die "a hero's death." He's watched friends

and fellows die those.

In the Burmese forest, to distract himself, he invents whole fantasy futures with girls he's never met, girls who probably wouldn't choose him anyway. It's always been like that with him. He's always looked different. Neither this, nor that. But when shelling starts in the forests of Nhpum Ga, and there's nowhere to go from that impossible bluff of mountain—his company, the 2d Battalion of the Marauders, has already been there five days—his heart begins to turn to ash, thinking he'll never be with a girl again, at all. The Japanese are all around, shelling constantly. Heavy casualties. Words that sound just like words until they happen around you.

'Never' too is a word like a bullet with the range of infinity. What can it possibly mean? The 2d Battalion's perimeter—400 by 250 yards on top of a 2,800-foot-high saddle of ground that dominates the surrounding terrain—is filling with shit and gangrene. At night the forest smells like the collective fear and rage of the men marooned on the bluff. That smell will never leave Amherst fully. Also the smell of agony, longing, and vomit. The men sleep and wake fitfully, or not at all. Their suffering feels like airlessness rather than pain.

Then the Japs capture the waterhole. Then Amherst and a few others like him—yellow men, Americans with Asian mixed in—start to be sent out at dead of night to try and bring back water. The second time, Amherst's mate Sterling gets shot down. He has to leave Sterling (father's name Tanaka, mother American, old San Francisco family) at the hole. He just barely gets back himself.

They don't talk about death. Or about relief. Or about home. Or about girls, apple pie, or football games. By silent pact. Among the many pacts that men fighting and dying together make with one another. They can no longer bear it, but there's nothing they can do, they have to bear it. They bear it.

On the ninth morning—Amherst is keeping track of the days for no reason he can name—Robby Mook points his index finger upward at the sky. Deakins, with a foot already turning a mottled, marbled maroon from where he stepped on some shrapnel two days ago, groans and rubs his eyes. Amherst will remember as if it's a movie he watched. Though the sun is barely visible through the trees above, bits and pieces of a leaden sky can be seen, and the occasional plane cuts through the patchy gray-blue like a silver arrow. They've run out of water two days ago. The waterhole is in the crosshairs of the Japanese a few hundred feet away and below, and even if you slither to it like a worm you risk getting a nice, thwacking bullet in your noggin as you try to dip your makeshift water bag into the stinking, crusted water. Sterling and his maggots are keeping guard at the approach. Case in point. His body probably is still there. Has Sterling's blood mixed with the hole's water? Probably.

And then Robby says, "Look, fellas, look!" He tries to buck upward but can't. Keeps pointing up, though, looking as if he's giving the sky the wrong finger.

"Aww, pipe down, would'ya?" Someone a few bodies away grunts. And then the water bags start dropping.

Planes like angels have brought relief; manna has dropped from heaven. Robby Mook is shuddering and weeping, rolling on the wet ground toward the bags as they fall. Stray Japanese bullets from below blow a few bags into

silver showers. There's shouting and yeehawing and whooping. There's sobbing and retching.

Amherst can only think that Sterling won't be needing any water . . . he's quite dead. In a few minutes the bags stop falling, the droning and the planes go away, but they're alive and it's morning and they know they might live, at least another day. They are the company to be famous later as Merrill's Marauders. Howdy, goddammit. Some of them say they are the 'Fightin' Aggies.' They say 'whoop' a lot. Still alive on that hilltop. A bunch of men in raggedy clothes, stringy hair, and dead eyes, dancing jigs and back-slapping each other.

And then on the eleventh day the 1st and 3rd battalions break through to them. They find broken men who have aged years, not days, during the siege. Lucky for Amherst and Robby and Deakins; Sterling is just plain ole dead.

Amherst gets back to a Calcutta that is sloppy with rain—the usual. That city has a way of weeping weakly for messy mankind. Huge craters have opened up on the roads. Traffic crawls. He has quite a time shutting out an image of Sterling's face turning into the face of an ancient man. Sterling sort of rolled like a log a few times when the Japanese sniper guard took him down. Amherst can't forget the healthy cream of Sterling's face draining faster than he thought possible. It reminds him of his mother when she was dying. Her skin, too, creased and puckered. Like a much older woman's skin. Gray, not creamy, tired from cancer pain. The colors, smells, the final bloated still shape of death, have never faded either.

In Calcutta, he knows he has to look sharp and keep things going. The city is a wild place. He is a wild man. He tries to construct some sense of a shape of things. In spite of the blur that will continuously creep up. Every day. From different directions. Like an eclipse. Sometimes he just sits. Waits. For darkness to pass. For something to happen. For someone to come. To be called for a meal. Some days he drinks till he blacks out. Some days he stays in bed. The smells and sounds of the Nhpum Ga forest stay with him. Days are still a fretwork of jumping light and shadow, nightmare and guilt. Nights are a primeval forest.

When someone asks him that certain question, with that certain raised eyebrow and smart-alecky face, he says he's Chinese, Chinese American.

He has to live. He must move. Standing before the dressing mirror in his bare billet on Lansdowne Road, he runs his hand through his coarse hair. An old nervous gesture. He's going out. His hair used to be light brown; a nothing color, like his skin. In school he pulled it back with a comb and put a good bit of his mother's pomatum on it so that he'd have a wider, broader forehead. Look more Anglo. Nice. Normal. Now it's sunburnt almost to an ashy bracken.

He has his mother's slanting, almost black eyes, but his face is longer and leaner, like his father's. His father's long face ends in a sharply cleft chin. He has no cleft. His chin is bulbous.

He's not a pretty sight. There are violet hollows under his eyes. His Adam's apple pokes out alarmingly. He also needs a shave. Because he's alive. When

you're alive, hair grows. Nails too. He clips his nails. What about Sterling?
Still lying there on that alien soil? Is it sunny? Rotting down to bone? Didn't
someone say once that hair and nails grow even on corpses? For a while . . .

Why didn't they pick Sterling up when they left? He should've asked. He
should've insisted.

He and Sterling used to pretend that they shaved almost every day, like the
other fellows.

Mongol. Mongrel. Yellow Peril.

They'd heard those words in school, in the streets, back home. Whispered,
flung at them, as they expected. They took them in stride. They were not surprised. That was the key thing. Not to be surprised or look surprised. They
didn't talk back.

The teachers wouldn't listen to them. Sometimes even a teacher made fun
of their accent.

"Say 'lyrical,' " the English teacher shouted.

"Rirical."

"L-y-ri-cal!"

"Ree-ri-cal."

"Imbecile!"

They didn't talk back in the army either. The commander told them to
act like men. "Cuz you fellers are . . . you know . . . Yellers!" And he burst into
thigh-slapping laughter at his own joke, giving the cue to the other men.

Today, it having rained a lot, the Calcutta sun feels kind. Moist, warm air
feels kind too. These days a few ocean liners still pull in and out of city docks,
loading and unloading batches of—among other things—men and women fresh
from Britain. Some are already wilted or withered. But fresh young girls from
England are still coming, though less and less. Looking for husbands. He has
no chance with them.

There are cars everywhere. He sees Baby Austins, Chevrolets, Packards
and army jeeps taking daredevil chances. Horns blare. Tires screech as the
inevitable pedestrian tempts death. Women in shiny pencil heels traipse in and
out of department stores.

Amherst tries to breathe in the day, the light, the air, the sounds—shrill
bird-cries of rickshaw pullers, vendors, and the occasional palanquin bearer—
as deeply as possible. At Nhpum Ga there were times when he'd stop breathing
because he was scared the Japs would hear it. This city, this white Calcutta,
is paradise by comparison. But maybe not for too long. The curious, knowing
'black' city prowls right outside. Always has. India for Indians. It's 1942. The
Quit India movement leaves streets littered with lathis, turbans, flags, posters,
the occasional body waiting to be removed.

And, he notices, more and more people begging in the streets. Their bodies
are unusually still, only the hands lifted in pleading. Makes them look like thin,
dark birds with long necks and tiny heads.

Today he has an invitation to the Calcutta Club from an old acquaintance. Sunny Roy. He's an 'old' acquaintance because everything before the dank Burmese forest seems eons ago. General wheeler-dealer and playboy from a respectable old Calcutta family. Born Saurendra Roy. Nice fellow, though too fond of the sauce and a fop and, sometimes Amherst suspects, a pansy. He wonders what Sunny Roy's father thinks of his son.

Leaving his taxi, he squints even at the mild midafternoon sun. Things, men, the air itself, are scrubbed into flickering, glassy ghosts. Something has happened to his vision. He doesn't see very clearly anymore, especially not up close. Faces blur and bob as he nears them. Something went wrong in those days of damp, freezing rain, squelching mud, shit crawling with leeches, and fear unlike anything he has ever known. Blinding fear, as they say. Blinding fear in those days when he was always picked for waterhole runs and scouting. The chaps caught glimpses of the enemy in him. He doesn't blame them, exactly. He understands. He never refused. But his eyes haven't readjusted to warmth, food, shelter, and safety. They remain scratchy; his vision remains blurred. Maybe a blood vessel burst. Maybe worse. He accepts it; he accepts most things, never sure of the ground on which he stands anywhere, anyhow. Since a boy he's known not to resist, to do as told.

He hasn't seen the army surgeon in Calcutta. He doesn't want to be told that he's going blind or something. He doesn't think you can avoid suffering. Where's there to go when harm seeks you out? Maybe this is the Oriental in him.

The army was his ticket away from his father. He didn't leave his mother unprotected. She'd died. Finally at rest. At peace. He hopes. She used to say that her life was her fate. It used to make him angry. After Nhpum Ga he's come to see things a lot more her way. There's no escaping fate. His vision's damaged. Okay.

He's seen such things. A man might well put out his own eyes after that. At least he can still see into the distance. Maybe the army will still have some use for him. At least—the sting of this whip is familiar, almost stabilizing—he's better off than Sterling.

CHAPTER 55

He finds Sunny—ever loyal to pleasure-seeking—waiting for him at the imposing entrance to the Calcutta Club. Sunny stands at the club's neo-Palladian entrance, a drink already swanky between his fingers. Sunny is—as always—dressed in the nattiest possible nattiness: seersucker jacket, white panama, the jauntiest of jaunty pearl-gray spats. . . . He'd say a sight for sore eyes, but . . . smiles a little at his own thought.

Sunny's about five feet four, pale and splotchy from habitual drinking and fast living. Probably going a little pulpy inside. Not a handsome man. A *pukka*

brown sahib. A crumpled half pack of *Gauloises* is peeping out of his front pocket.

"Passel of smart new gals today in the club, old chap," he says. His voice is a quaver. Always has been.

Amherst feels lustful and lonely.

Such sets will always be exotic, fascinating, and condescending to him. People will take one look at his yellowish-pink complexion, do a double take, and not know what to say or not want to say what they're thinking. Or they'll try to be nonchalant and overfriendly. But Amherst always feels that he can hear them thinking, "Yellow man in American standards!! A Yankee Jap!!!"

He always wants to be invisible till he can tell what kind of reception he will get. Him, half Japanese. There are yellow cowards, yellow fever, yellow journalism. These days there are yellow men, the newest minted and certified menace to humanity. One of the many kinds of yellow peril. Inside the club everyone looks darker, but skin is skin and blood is blood. Those who come to this club also usually have lifelong training in reading pedigree, moreover. Amherst's father is a plumber.

He fears—he fantasizes—that he might be put into the state of mere brute: panting, imbecile, mongrel, neither this nor that, neither friend nor foe, neither brown nor white. In some sort of battle royal. Just a freak. Fear, being shapeless, expands infinitely. At Nhpum Ga or at Calcutta Club.

Sunny introduces him to people who shake his hand warmly. Their eyes shine. Is he a hero then, after all? His father always says a blush is revolting on yellowing cream skin.

He sees a woman sitting at the far end of the Crystal Room at the mahogany bar. She's perfectly poised and sitting quite still. She doesn't stir or change her expression when Sunny begins guiding Amherst that way, a light pressure of his hand on Amherst's elbow. When he's close to her, he looks as steadily and long as he dares.

Delicate ankles disappearing into shiny red high-heeled pumps. Pale egg-shaped calves, a little plump. His imperfect gaze travels up to her pale pink skirt and then the many-ringed hand holding a drink. Her soft white blouse is like that of a schoolgirl, but its low-buttoned front draws men's eyes to peeking cleavage. He feels dizzy.

She's introduced to him as Jolene. Anglo-Indian. Poor thing. One of his sort. While she says hello politely but coolly he wants to reach out and stroke the curve of her cheek.

That night he looks at himself in his tiny bathroom mirror, close and long. He's tipsy, or giddy, or happy, can't say. All he knows is that he's met a girl he can't stop thinking about.

No, it isn't because he hasn't been with a girl in a long while. Or it isn't just that. In fact, he's also never been with any girl for long, but that isn't it. It's her.

They're both mongrels, this girl and he. They know that world of no particular, real roots. They're both despised by both sides of their lineage, no fault of theirs. Suspect, strays by birth. He looks at his poor straight hair sticking up despite all his efforts to smooth it down; his nose—he finds it revolting—wide,

flat. He was nicknamed Genghis Khan in school. . . . Suppose his could be the wind-cracked face of that tiny yellow man on horseback in the old paintings where everyone looks like a bird? Slashing at some enemy with a sword as large as himself. Had Genghis Khan's father beaten him regularly when he was a boy? Amherst knows battle, of course. And killing. Sometimes he thinks he should pray for the enemy he's butchered. Rows and rows of Japanese boys— just the same yellow as him—coming at him, at the Marauders. Row after row, mowed down, not stopping. *"Banzai!"* A volley. Again. "Banzai!" And again. The hot, rusty smell of blood.

How people see him or Jolene has so little to do with their real lives.

But he's alive. Sterling isn't.

So next day he calls up Sunny. Asks him if he can come to the club again. The club admission rules are very strict—it's not really a place for people like him. He tells Sunny he'd like to have a chance to see Jolene again. Sunny is all chuckles and guffaws.

"Certainly, dear chap, certainly . . . quite a girl, quite a girl . . . ," he keeps saying as Amherst tries to hang up the coin-operated phone in the drafty, wide hallway of his temporary billet.

So he goes again. She smiles when she sees him, making his heart jump against his ribs. When she smiles it's a slow, almost mocking smile. He nearly turns back, scared by his louche need. That evening he sits with her at the bar, elbows almost touching.

He notices her hair is a dark, almost squid-ink blue. Dye job, he thinks. But a nice one. It's pushed away from her face and clusters in tight curls around her ears. He watches her mouth, her tiny even teeth, the pink tip of her tongue, her neck, her collarbone as she talks and turns her head this way and that, looking at people coming and going, waving at someone in another part of the room. He is fairly sure she's warming under the heat of his frank gaze, his cataloging of her beauty. The side of her neck with a dark mole on it is excruciatingly fragile, unbearably vulnerable. He wants to lick the mole, the neck. Two little gold balls gleam on her earlobes. Poppy-red lipstick.

She seems accustomed to looking, gauging, boring, sizing up. Used to judging closeness, intention, the smallest of movements, moves. He desperately wants to put his arm around her shoulders, to protect her. He guesses that she's had a short childhood.

When she looks him full in the eye, he nearly topples over, her eyes are so dark and he's had so many whiskies on Sunny. Then, just as the back of his head is about to hit the floor, he finds himself swimming in her dark pupils instead.

A group of young women come up to Jolene and begin chattering. They give him not unfriendly looks up and down, almost appreciative. He isn't used to tolerance, leave alone appreciation. It goes to his head where he's already swimming alone like a quick fish in a crater lake at night.

Things are going to turn, he thinks.

"Will you monopolize our Jolene all evening, lieutenant?" one of the women teases not unkindly. Trying to look sober, Amherst grins like an idiot, looks for Sunny, sees him across the room, goes off that way. As he leaves, fighting his stumble, Jolene winks at him.

"Smitten, eh?" Sunny asks him. He has to have several coffees to try and sober up. His heart is galloping.

Sunny doesn't, can't know the half of it.

Some more banter with Sunny. Some men are reading out details of a siege that just happened in Myitkyina. Chaps hacking holes in their pants to let the dysentery flow while they load and fire their guns at the crazy Banzai boys. Chaps falling asleep at their guns from exhaustion and hunger only to have the Japanese creep up to their lines and blow their heads off. Fifteen hundred American boys dead, the count mounting.

He's desperate to find that magic spell again, to put his hands around that crystal ball of desire, that magic globe, like warm paws; keep it safe. It looks like it might begin to disintegrate.

Who am I? he thinks. Maybe he says it aloud. Patriot? Traitor? Who the hell am I?

Just then he sees her walk past, so plumed yet so fragile.

You're lucky, Amherst you scoundrel, he thinks. You got away. You are in the Calcutta Club. Drinking the best bourbon, no doubt a salute to your country for oh so recently joining the fight. In a room with bright light, cool air, plenty to eat and drink. Beautiful women. You are alive, fella. In one piece. A pretty gal called Jolene is here, very close.

But then the sharp twist he felt in his gut when the water-run call came on the bluff comes back. Civilians are excitedly discussing the war and the battles. He is unspeakably lonely. Men of his company have been pressed back into the frontlines, he learns. They must be dying even then of dysentery, cholera, typhoid, scrub fever, gangrene, a shot to the head. Now he imagines, against his will, fighting the images, the Myitkyina men's faces, their hollow eyes. Eyes smoky with hate or rage or simply exhaustion—he can't tell. And Sterling's dead.

But.

He is here.

That's when he makes up his mind.

Why wait? One day the war will end. Who knows what new storm will gather that day? Who knows what that age will bring? Who knows what India will be? Will the British give her independence? Who knows? If not, will India shatter into a thousand pieces? Will Hindus and Muslims hack each other to death?

He'll be gone, surely. Juniper and ash again; the smell of eucalyptus. The sky a tall blue arch overhead. California. The gentle waves of the Pacific, cresting softly, crashing gently. Pale gold, sandy beaches. When the war ends, he doesn't want Jolene to be alone in India. He's seen the black looks people are giving one another on the streets already. He's heard about the killings here

and there, everywhere. Gandhi fasts each time killing breaks out, and it stops for a bit. Gandhi sits up, drinks a glass of lemon juice with honey, and the killing starts again.

The English watch, wait . . . waver? They're taking their time.

To free or not to free.

And he's waiting too to be free from his memories, his nightmares. Free to pursue happiness. To not be alone.

Well, he's not English. He's American. He's not going to wait. He's going make a quick call.

Sometimes everything a man feels is absolutely, 100 percent real. Every nightmare is real. Every imaginary whisper is real. Now is his time to make love as if love has been discovered for the first time. This is the way of his times, a time of keeping what one can find. This is love now.

"Hey Amherst! Look sharp, old chap. We're off to play a game of billiards till supper time . . . join us old boy, won't you?" Sunny punches his arm roughly. Sunny's English toff talk amuses him. He goes with him.

When he sees Jolene again—she's sipping champagne from a slender fluted glass—he goes up to her and asks for a dance. She leaves the bar, quite at ease, her hand resting lightly on his arm. The band is jamming something jazzy. They dance. She's quiet. He's nervous. Afterwards they stand smoking in the gardens. The moon is high in the sky and the garden lamps twinkle through the trees. The air is not dull with anguish and pain; it's just the soft, moist breath of the Bay of Bengal.

Time. Of the essence. If he doesn't move fast someone else will snap her up. There are too many men hanging about the clubs, restaurants and bars of Calcutta, pockets clinking, eyes glistening. Pretty girls have their choice.

He asks her to marry him.

"Tell me, Lieutenant. Buck, do you even know my last name?" She says 'Left-e-nant,' like the Brits.

He attempts gallantry. "Won't you be changing it to mine?"

She smiles patiently. His attempt to be fresh. She has surely heard it all.

"But you don't know it. And you're asking me to marry you?"

He gropes, hopelessly, for a witty, gallant retort. He pushes back his hair, rubs his big, ugly nose.

Before it gets too awkward—though Jolene is still smiling at him—sounds of applause come from the club. Louder music comes to them through the club's open windows. The band's playing "We'll meet again, don't know where, don't know when . . ."

The notes of Vera Lynn's cockney contralto fill the air. The audience is singing along. Sunny trots over, pointing out the obvious. "It's a BESA night! What fun, eh old boy?!!" BESA—the Bengal Service Entertainment Association—has been contracted to play tonight at the club as a special treat. Maybe another minor skirmish not gone horribly wrong. Maybe a sudden offhand

noblesse oblige of the generals.

Sunny sways from side to side, belting out "We'll meet again . . . ," with a girl on each arm: spritzy, feisty. Unsteady, unsober. Joyous. If his is a gutter-snipe kind of joy, it is uncomplicated, easy.

For Amherst, yellow son of a father furiously disappointed in the conse-quences of lust, such easy joy is not possible. He was shoved to the frontlines by his father's hot, meaty hand, no questions asked. His father had shoved him also into football in high school where a fall and a blow left him with a ringing in one ear that came back on the bluff. His father marched him up to the war recruiting office in 1941—"'ere's a red-blooded American boy wantsa take out a few Japs"—and saw him off on his battleship.

Mongrel. Japanese Suzie from San Francisco and Anglo-Saxon Ambrose from 'down-deep' Kentucky somehow got together in Los Angeles and brought him into an America that spits him out daily like gristle in an otherwise perfect cut of meat.

He is furious, been furious, all his life. That is why he wants another story. He must have it. He wants a happy ending, two worlds mingling, not clashing.

Sunny—bless his soul—shrieks and whistles at a brief pause in the melody, making the entire room whoop and bellow. Do these people know what they're really doing? What's really going on? For fuck's sake, this is a little war dance, is it? Jolene and he find themselves a few feet to lean on against a wall—now it is standing room only—and listen.

Someday they'll be gone as if they never lived, loved, laughed, or fought. They'll be ghosts staring out of yellowing photos at people trying to imagine—or maybe not—what their lives were like.

He doesn't want children himself but some of them, maybe, will be the children of the dancers and drunks here tonight. Maybe they will or maybe they won't realize that the frail, antique-looking people in the old photos had been real people, quite like them, and also different. That they bled when they were cut. Just like them. That they were flesh and blood. Weak and brave. Maybe they'll even imagine this night of warm Bay of Bengal breezes and lemony-gold chandelier light. This moment. This happy moment! Maybe they who are living in this moment will never truly be dead to the ones to come.

He wishes those children well, and he believes in them. Though that night he can't see their faces, though they too are ghosts of the future, unknown, unborn, he wishes them long life, happy memories, wonder, and delight.

Because there is still magic left in the world.

Like Vera Lynn's song.

The dancers flow around him and Jolene like a flock of swallows. Jolene puts her hand in his at some point, and he holds it firm, sure—and hoping—that there will be blue skies "some sunny day.

Part 8:

Swing Time, Darjeeling, 1943–

CHAPTER 56

Prem goes to Roma's room with every intention of saying the right thing, making the right sense, being wise and comforting. She rehearses her little speech as she goes. It holds together as she goes. Yet, in Roma's bedroom she finds she can't string the words together as she intended. They won't fall into order and hold up the same banner, the same banter of meaning.

So she feels torn between what she has come to say and what she wants to say. She wants to say, "Get up, my girl, and look out your window. There's a new dawn. The light is a slanting caress on the grass. You are young yet. You have loved and lost someone whom it was an honor to love."

Instead she says, "How are you feeling, my dearest girl?"

After Roma turns her head away to that very window, beyond which the sun has risen as usual—wound up by the divine clockmaker, with no choice in the matter for her, as Roma sees it—sitting at the very edge of the bed, near Roma's feet, noticing as if for the first time how scrawny, how petite Roma is, Prem tells her that a marriage proposal has come for her.

For a few seconds Roma doesn't move. Then she turns her head to look at Prem, her eyes clear and wide as if she has just seen the sun rise for the first time.

"Mashimoni, please."

"What, my dear?"

"Please never bring this up again."

Prem stares mutely in anguish.

"How will you live my dear? I won't live forever."

"I don't want to live Mashimoni."

"Don't say that, Roma." Prem leans slightly forward, taking care not to breach too much the distance between herself and Kanan's daughter. A girl she's never fully understood. And always tried to love in spite of it.

"Mashimoni, can't I just stay here the way I am? No one wants me, really. I've been lucky. I've had you, and Harish, and . . . Roderick. But my luck has run out, Mashimoni. Can't you just let me stay? Just the way we are now, the way things are. I don't want anything more, Mashimoni."

Prem lowers her head and fights back tears. Her body—every hard and soft place in it—is weary of crying. She would crash but for the fact that there's no one else to hold up this world she built so painfully. Now she takes a pellet at least once a day. Some of the servants whisper and stare sometimes; she knows. The spine of the great Mitter edifice wobbles as she wobbles. She ignores the stares and whispers; she has to get through the days and nights. Everyone needs her. With the malice of a repetitive injury, grief corrodes her bones and tissues a little more every time she cries. This is why, perhaps, she herself has

mostly finished crying. She accepted within a few days that Roderick was dead. But Roma held out so long. She wishes she hadn't allowed that. If only she'd shaken Roma out of that fantasy, then and there.

And if only Roderick hadn't gone and died.

If she could have, she would have offered Roma a pellet. But she can't. She must not.

Please. I tried.

"You can't say that, darling. You're still young. You have so much time ahead of you."

"Mashimoni, please don't say that. Stop saying that. I wish I were dead, Mashimoni. I wish I were dead. I wish I'd died that day when I went out on that march against the Simon Commission. Remember? You scolded me so much that day. Now, if I hadn't come back at all you wouldn't have had to—"

"Can't keep looking back, child—"

"Why not? They used to say I killed my mother; you know that, right? My own father flung me to you when I was small. And I haven't seen him in years, right? See? My own father didn't love me. You think I've forgotten that? You can't ask me not to look back. Now there's no future also . . ."

Roma cries so hard that she hiccups for an hour afterward. Prem, who took a little bit of a pellet before she came, stays seated at the foot of the bed, her head against a bedpost, her eyes half-closed.

That may be the first day in the six months that Roma has refused to leave her room that she really cries. She doesn't cry only for the fallen hero, though she cries for him too. She cries for the what might-have-beens of the life she's lived thus far. For what might have been if her mother had lived. For what might have been if her father, though poor and weak, had loved her. For what might have been, what choices she might have had, if she'd been beautiful, movie star material. If Roderick had lived and they had married.

Because all that imaginary fulfillment, that vindication has turned out to be a purely unattainable dream, like the one in which she's Roderick's wife and taking her poor gaunt mother shopping. She cries from self-pity, from the shock of the violated narcissist, from the fright of seeing the story of her disappointment as the handwriting of fate on the face of an indifferent universe.

Harish comes to speak to her. "Didi, do you want to go somewhere? Let's go to Darjeeling, Didi. We need to leave the city for a while, don't you think?" The first few times he comes and talks she stays in bed, on her side, her back turned to him. But then one day she thinks, Why not? What is here for me after all?

She has looked at the piece of world outside her window coming into focus and going out of it for months. Though she doesn't fully want to admit it, the scene tires her now. She would like at least to wake up to a different picture outside her window. She would like to, maybe, see snow, and mountains, and fir trees. Maybe she would like to walk along winding hill roads. Like a romantic heroine.

Part 8: Swing Time, Darjeeling, 1943–

And she doesn't know this, but this mood is her salvation. She can live for the imagination of novelty better than for anything else. She can best force herself into activity propelled not by purpose, but by nothing more nor less than boredom. The disappointed grief of Roderick remains wrapped around her senses and her heart like dark, cancerous tentacles, but the only thing that can maybe dull that grinding, choking sensation—maybe—is appetite for a new palette, a new image, a new panorama.

To Darjeeling they go.

Prem is happier than she dares show, for fear that sharing the excitement of this moment might somehow make Roma grow moody again, make her rethink the moment itself. When the car leaves for the airport with Roma and Harish in the back seat and his valise and her suitcase in the trunk, Prem wants to cry for relief. She can't, so she sinks down onto the chaise in her parlor and dozes for a little while.

Darjeeling, the favorite Himalayan summer resort of the British, rivaled only by Shimla further north, is regularly rocked these days by sensational rumors about imminent invasion by the Japanese, but now that America is in the war no one pays great heed to these rumors, the general mood is upbeat, and insouciance and conviviality, a feisty *joie de vivre*, prevails just as the news from Burma and Singapore becomes more and more dire. Thousands massacred. Stories of atrocities committed on civilians, POWs and Buddhist monks alike. The Japanese are building a road to the north to cut off crucial supplies to China and Malaysia, grinding their POWs to death in the forced labor camps where the road is being built.

Maybe the conviviality is a *danse macabre*. Maybe not. It's a strange swing time. Darjeeling's clubs and private bungalows overflow with revelers. Servicemen, tea gardeners, nurses and medical staff, some of the top brass of the American and British armies in the China-Burma war theatre, drink it up and live it down. Jazz and ragtime float out of brightly lit buildings. The buildings are so crowded, gay, that they seem to throb and glow. The liquor is plentiful, thanks mostly to the Americans, and the storied hospitality of tea planters to their own kind is at its apogee. Mixed with the merriment is a thumbing the nose at death.

When Roma arrives here from the relatively ceremonious, staid world of Calcutta, her senses receive a jolt both salutary and shocking. Calcutta, until lately the British capital of India, articulates tragedy as well as everyday life in high seriousness only. For example, Roderick used to play football on the side of the Bengal team—barefoot and unprotected from the punishing cleats of the British teams as the Bengali players had to be, but by his own choice—and the story has done its rounds so many times since his disappearance that it has attained mythic status. In Darjeeling people seem to—at least claim to—live for the day, the night, the moment, the martini. Here all the grandiosity of the Quit India movement's as yet disappointing failure fails to deter most people

from drinking to the perdition of Hitler and Mussolini every night, and for some also through most of the day.

Roma and Harish are staying in the bungalow of Chandan Sen, an old schoolmate of Harish and son of planters who own the bungalow. Chandan is in Darjeeling on the ice-thin pretext of learning to manage his family's tea garden. He is a good sport, as the Brits and Americans at the clubs say. He's a charming and guileless member of the exploitative class but the tea garden doesn't do so well under his nominal management. There are rumors about blind intoxication and certain liberties taken with plantation workers' womenfolk. But since these rumors arise from humble shacks and work-hardened organs, it is them against Chandan who, it must at least be granted, is a jolly good fellow. Some youthful indiscretions, yes, the club matriarchs—for there are those even among the Bacchae—concede, but then what young man hasn't sowed wild oats in the past, and what young man in the myriad brave new ages to come won't?

Roma discovers a new pleasure in life: alcohol.

She and Chandan, in fact, grow jolly and chummy over Roma's ability—discovered and trumpeted by Chandan—to drink most people under the table. Harish watches and worries some, but is just too glad to see Roma finally emerge from the darkness of the last year to say much. And in any case they will be returning to Calcutta soon.

Roma is, in fact, a sturdy drinker. An uncharitable observer would perhaps, again, invoke a comparison with that father now lost in the mists of time, but Roma in her cups is guilty of no significant indignities or excesses, at least as of yet. So she dips her sorrows in drink but always swims across to the other shore named survival, and this can only be encouraging and comforting to those who love her and believe her newly gained lust for life to be a ladder, not a pit.

About two weeks after arrival in Darjeeling, Roma announces to Harish that she and Chandan are engaged. Harish, stunned, briefly remonstrates, urges delay. But then he thinks that Didi and Chandan seem well paired, in fact, in many ways. They even seem happy together. Harish sees no reason to demur, to stand in the way, in the end. After all, Didi has suffered enough. And Chandan, wild oats and all, is really a good sport in the end. A week later Calcutta high society learns that Roma Chatterjee has accepted marriage overtures from the rich tea-planter parents of a certain Chandan Sen, Esq., and because Sir Naren has had a third stroke that has left him without speech or movement, his son Harish Mitter gives her away.

CHAPTER 57

The new Mr. and Mrs. Sen live in a house overlooking the Green Valley tea plantation. In morning mist, when smoke rings of clouds fight back the weak, newborn sun, the tiered *terai* beneath looks like the exuberant frills of a green skirt some whimsical girl has left on the hillside. The house was once painted a sky blue, with white trim on the windows and doors. Now its misty grayish exterior blends in with the hills rather nicely. The center of the house, presiding over the terai, is colonial bungalow: the rest of it—servants' quarters, storeroom, packaging room and business office—sprawls languidly on either side.

In the evenings a long shiny car, with many dents and scratches on it, drives up to the bungalow. The little figure at the tip of its bonnet dances ecstatically before it becomes a still piece of metal. Chandan gets out of the car, grappling with the door, especially if he is a bit plastered.

Roma doesn't love him. As to him, what counts as love for him is hard to say. He is an essentially good-natured man. Feckless, terrible with money, sentimental, gullible, but good-natured. But somehow the meaning of married love for him is largely uncomplicated coexistence. He likes Roma's company; he likes her liking for liquor. As to the marriage, in part it is a bargain he has struck with his parents—Roma does not know that—who have been trying to push him into marriage for a while because of rumors that float back to them from the hills. That he gets unruly and sometimes nasty when really drunk, has certainly slept with some of his female workers and who knows who else. There probably are a few unclaimed children fathered by him growing up around the bungalow, in the hills, in neighboring gardens and bungalows. This sort of behavior is not in general unusual among the planters who feel liberated both by distance from Calcutta, and by the whiff of high living and gaiety, and life as either party or auction, as traditional in British plantocracy.

Roma is grateful her in-laws don't live with them. They stay in Calcutta in their flat on Park Street. The flat is rumored to be mortgaged to a rich *Marwari* entrepreneur. But such secret or not-so-secret bankruptcies and mortgages to owners of filthy lucre are not unheard of among high society in Calcutta.

Here in Darjeeling it is a cotton candy pink cloud world; here the line between reality and fantasy is usually blurred by choice. Somehow this suits Roma very well. She likes the feeling of being on a constant high. Drinks at lunch and dinner and until long into the ringing, echoing night; parties every night, sometimes several the same night; apparently enough money to feel unconcerned about the present or the future (the past, now that's a different matter); and an unabashed pursuit of excessive pleasures or perhaps just lazy self-indulgence. She welcomes, even, this low flame existence after the years

of smoldering grief. Chandan and she get along very well together. As for love and intimacy, they manage. As every other woman or wife probably manages, she's convinced. She's a respectably, comfortably married woman now, and nosy gossipmongers can just stay guessing if they must poke their heads into other people's business.

Her everyday life here is not that different from that in Calcutta, moreover. There is a continuum of idleness and being waited upon hand and foot between the two places and times that characterizes affluence as well as its ghostly imposter. Dinner at home, though rare, is at eight, with its rituals. There's watery soup, some sort of poached fish or bird, collapsing carrots, peas and tomatoes for vegetables, and some fruit compote for dessert. The sort of food they eat is what the cook—a grumpy old Nepali man—used to serve the English family who owned the place until 1935. It's posh food; English food.

Roma thinks she should try her hand at cooking. Chandan tells her it's *infra dig*; his mother will have a fit if she hears about Roma in the kitchen. Still, since she's got the bee in her bonnet, she persists. She's in the kitchen at four in the afternoon, making the cook's helper grind turmeric and cumin, chop tomatoes, make mustard paste. It's all guesswork, but it comes along. Old Jung Bahadur the cook stands by, his face a study in fury. But that food turns out inedible. The curries are watery, the vegetables soggy, the rice burnt. Frustrated, she grinds the spices herself, chops vegetables, soaks the rice beforehand. The food comes out gritty, full of sand, oversalted. Chandan leaves the table in a huff and drives off to the club, just a slight edge of meanness showing through in him for the first time.

Then Roma realizes that Jung Bahadur is personally tampering with the food before it's served. He's mixing dirt, sand, whatever, into prepared dishes. If she wants to have her cooked food served, she'll have to stand in the kitchen when it's being cooked and served instead of sitting at table like the lady of the house. Jung Bahadur will reduce her to that before he gives up his rule over the kitchen. She fires him. The next day none of the staff come to work. She washes her hands of the matter. She will not let servants' well-known saboteur methods spoil her life now.

Chandan says, "Didn't I tell you?"

Roma, sipping a whiskey sour while turning the pages of a fashion magazine, looks at him, frowning slightly, then decides to say nothing and also wipes the frown off her face quickly because she thinks frowning accentuates her plainness.

From then on they eat boiled and braised meat and fish, tasteless side dishes, and watery desserts to round things out when they do eat at home.

But then, something that might have been expected happens. Over a week or so, Roma feels that she can't really taste anything. And when the unborn child makes its existence known a few weeks later, Roma sobs unconsolably. Chandan isn't elated either; he makes perfunctory motions of solacing her while he sits—for the first time in months—at home, nursing his normally peripatetic bourbon.

And then something strange happens. Roma begins to wrap herself around

the unborn child, almost unwittingly. Though she's terrified about giving birth, feeling nearly dead at the very idea, recalling the terrifying things she's heard about it. Her mother died giving birth to her.

What was her mother like? She existed, after all. Before the Mitters, before the newborn universe emptied out, before her own eyes opened, a young, utterly unprepared girl had a baby and died. Roma had supposedly killed her. Will her own child kill her? She asks herself if, as she lay dying, her mother sensed her baby outside her, felt for her even with cold, numb fingers, cried knowing she would never meet her daughter. Her father's mother—the only grandmother she's known—used to say her mother was a nothing, a weakling. Quickly snapped. Easily broken. Will she be like her mother?

She grows heavy with the child, and then surprisingly lighter of heart. She even begins to take morning walks because among the few dog-eared books the previous British owners left behind on a dusty shelf of what was once 'The Library,' she's come upon a certain Thomas Bull's *Hints to Mothers, For the Management of Health During the Period of Pregnancy, and in the Lying-Room; with an Exposure . . .* etc. Very long title. Cracked red leather binding, gilt lettering. Once a handsome book, obviously. Much thumbed. Sometimes she daydreams about the children who might have been born here. About the woman—the women? Englishwomen?—who relied on this book. Victorian Dr. Bull recommends walking. Sleep. Lots of rest. Roma leans considerably on him though of course she has her own living doctor, Dr. Ruggers, who has pretty much brought most of the better sort of hill babies into the world.

Then the day comes. Nothing could have prepared Roma for the birth or the darkness she feels after the birth. When a wailing thing is put in her arms by the midwife, she can barely hold it. "It's a girl," the midwife says. Her not unkind eyes seem to be saying, "What will you do?" Roma can feel nothing. She looks blankly at the splotchy, crunched-up face, the miniscule hands. The tiny twigs of fingers tinged red at the tips as if baby had to claw her way out of her. Which was how it felt.

Everything races. She falls asleep from exhaustion. She wakes to see again this little hatchling—utterly destructible, utterly powerful—next to her. She's taught to give her daughter the breast. It hurts a lot. When she feeds, and when she doesn't. The baby's choice. Roma's bondage.

Terror fills every inch of Roma. She's trapped—but this time she's done it to herself.

Look. At. What. I've. Done! she wants to scream.

What does she do now? Now that this child is the future's weathercock, its key in her tiny nipple-gripping beak.

Chandan sees the baby, squawks, wobbles, and leaves the house; he goes on a drinking spree. Roma is weakly furious. He doesn't return till almost forty-eight hours later. So she gets stuck with this creature that cries every hour or so, that even when asleep seems to want to butt back into her, that needs her body for food every few hours, that 'goes to the toilet' every few hours, that can't speak—can barely open its eyes—that's so tiny she's afraid to lift her, hold her.

She starts having a recurring dream. In her dream she cries out, reaches out, at sight of her mother and runs to her to keep her from disappearing behind a door. Always too late. By the time she gets close there's nothing but a door that opens onto nothing. And then she wakes up to the baby crying.

She attempts baby talk. Don't cry, baby, don't cry! My golden girl, my ray of moonlight, don't cry; there's no one like you in the world. But the baby keeps crying; nothing will stop it.

But what are lack of sleep, exhaustion, soreness, and burning breasts compared to the fear of not knowing who she's become?

What has she done? Really, what is this thing, this motherhood thing?

She doesn't have to wonder long.

The child dies.

In its crib, alone, at night.

This is what Roma can't forget, can't forgive herself for. That the child dies alone.

She worried so terribly that her baby would kill her. But instead the baby dies. All by herself. Apparently she just stopped breathing. When a baby all alone in a dark room feels death coming, does it have memories?

She thinks such things every waking hour and moment after this. She worries about the death of course, but even more about the fact that she wasn't there. She begins blaming herself for sleeping apart, with Chandan, in another room. An adjoining room, yes, but not the same room. Leave alone the same bed.

When she weeps on the trunk call Prem tries to calm her down. "Babies who sleep with their mother in the same bed also die like that suddenly sometimes, Roma. It wasn't your fault; it isn't anyone's fault. Don't cry anymore. It was meant to be." Should she tell Roma about other babies who died? Or nearly died? Or simply vanished? Does she herself believe that all those things were meant to be? She decides not to mention these things to Roma.

"No Mashimoni, there was fault! It was someone's fault! Nothing just happens just like that!! It was the crib that Chandan's parents gave us for her. Why did I listen? Why did I listen to them saying it was the better, modern way? Why didn't I keep my girl in bed with me?"

The girl had been named Rajani—Night—as perhaps fitting for a child of parents who were such boisterously nocturnal beings, but Roma doesn't want to say the name because its holder may have fought for air alone, in darkness, and lost.

Chandan's parents had in fact given the parents-to-be a crib. Within seconds of Roma or the nurse laying Rajani's tiny swaddled shape down in the too-large crib, the baby would let out a splintering wail so full of grief and disbelief that every time, Roma wanted to pick her up and stagger back to her bedroom and lay her down between herself and Chandan, however destroyed she felt. But she would always be held back by the nurse, and often asked by Chandan not to bring the child to bed. The nurse said, "Babies die when parents sleep on two sides. One of them rolls over and crushes the baby. Not safe."

Chandan said, "How can we possibly sleep with the baby in the bed?"

"The way you slept between your parents, that's how!"

"I never did," Chandan said, "That's my crib."

"Oh so your parents didn't even give their grandchild a new crib!"

"Why should they?" Chandan was unexpectedly sharp.

"Because they've given her this one thing, and it's not even new."

And Chandan said, his voice susurrous for the first time with contempt, "You don't know much about tradition and legacy, do you? Of course, how could you?"

This too. He could go wherever he pleased, whenever he pleased, with whomever he pleased, baby or no baby. She couldn't. She had to stay home with the baby. Alone. That was the worst thing. Chandan did often coo at and dote on the baby when he was home, but he still kept the hours he always had, and somehow it was her job alone to be a parent. A parent with a Nepalese Christian nurse in tow.

And it was that nurse who said that babies are safer in cribs. Roma tells her to leave at once. What else can she do? The penalty for the terrible mistakes she has made has to be entirely, remorselessly visited on people who should know better and didn't hold her back from her mistakes. She also has the crib burned before the bungalow in a big bonfire, and forces all the staff to stand around the fire as if it's a cremation. Why did her parents-in-law give her this death trap? When Chandan comes home that night the embers are still flickering, a little ash fluttering hither and thither. Of course the baby has already been gone a few days but this smoldering pyre reminds him so grotesquely, so scathingly, of the reality of the little body's succumbing to fire at the real cremation that he collapses on the wet, dark grass, and weeps.

When he enters the house some time later he hears a sound of something shattering. He doesn't investigate, just blindly gropes his way to the sofa in the family sitting room and falls asleep instantly. The next day there's a semi-expensive china vase in pieces on the floor. Also left behind by the English family. The broken edges don't even slightly hew to the lines of the images on the vase. All is rebellion. What the artist created over months—or maybe even years, who knows—has been returned to dust overnight.

Chandan too breaks into smaller and smaller pieces. One day Roma stumbles upon him nuzzling up against a young maidservant. One hand crushing her breast, the other upon the lintel of the bathroom door against which he has her pressed. Roma wants to look away, to turn around. Instead, she feels rooted to the spot. Standing a few feet away, just around the corner in a hallway that leads to the servants' bathroom, she watches her husband begin to force open another woman. The maid—just a girl, at most eighteen—stares at her over Chandan's shoulder, stricken, dry-eyed, mute. Chandan grinds himself against her, his face in her neck, upon the flat of her chest leading to the swell beneath, like a baby nuzzling, his back to Roma. He reeks even from where she stands.

And though Roma turns and flees from what she's seen, the horror of everything that's happened comes over her again, all at once. The anguish on the girl's face follows her. Anguish is anguish. Whether it's being taken without love by a drunken master, or a dead child, or a vanished hope. Everything burns

again in and around her. At night she lies awake, listening to the night pinging softly upon the hills here and there, its language obscure, its expanse unearthly.

Chandan starts drinking from about ten in the morning, doesn't stop till whatever wee hour he comes back from the club, and even then sometimes falls asleep with a tumbler of spilled whiskey rolling on the carpet near him. For weeks she lets him be. She thinks he should come to her. Because she can't. Since it was the crib. One morning, though, she does. She sits beside him on that old, overstuffed couch with its springs threatening to burst and impale the occupants. His eyes open and flutter, then land on her face. After a minute she asks, "Why?"

"I don't know," he says.

"Why won't you stay with me?"

He tries scrambling up, then gives up. The blood in his head is like a thousand drumbeats together. He wants to sleep. He doesn't want to be awake, to know of her need, her demands pressing on him.

Hoarsely, loudly he says, "Because you didn't do enough."

Roma stands up. "She cried for hours before she went to sleep each night. You don't know; you were drunk."

"You were the mother."

"What does that mean?"

"Ahha . . . I wish . . ." And he rolls over, turns his back to her and sinks into the most beautiful oblivion of all. She considers bashing his head in, raining down blows of the lit iron poker in the fireplace on his weak baby face.

One night she wakes up with a shudder. She can't say why. Her body feels something she doesn't know. Her fists are already clenched, fingernails digging into her palms. She looks at the space on the bed beside her. It is prim, unused, grayish—as usual. Chandan hasn't been to this bed for a while.

Nothing is different.

The sun taps on her closed eyes the next morning as, still in bed, she hears confused shouts, commands. The droning of an engine. Heavy steps clambering outside. She wonders what new devastation the cries and whimpers mean, but she doesn't want to leave the bed. It's so warm, so comforting. Then there is a pounding on the door. "Memshaab, memshaab, shaab . . . shaab is . . ."

She squeezes her eyes shut and feels the tears ooze out. Human, only too human. Tears of relief, grief, fatigue. For some reason she doesn't need to be told what's happening.

Outside, Chandan's body is stretched out on the verandah. His full height is apparent. He was over six feet tall. When did he shrink so much for her that she started thinking of him as a small man? A moral pigmy or something. . . .

Whoever cut him open from navel to sternum had to run up the buried knife a foot and then some. Though he's under a blanket, she hears of the nature of the wound from bystanders whispering. One or two make the sign of the cross. Several pairs of eyes are trained on her. They expect her to show

sorrow. She stares down at the puffy, broken-veined face of the corpse of her dead husband.

Mostly she feels disbelief. She almost wants to ask, "Why?" Is he really dead, or is he playing possum? Might he spring up as soon as she turns, grip her in a laughing hug?

Yes, Roma is afraid to turn. Things can change very quickly. Anything can happen. To any one, at any time. She knows that from intimate experience. No place is safe. But the corpse doesn't move. She can see that it isn't breathing. Chandan would have to be a great actor to pretend to be so still.

So tiring. All this death.

Chandan's really dead. Her knees weaken as she absorbs this.

The police come. She answers questions blankly, carelessly. The inspector means well; he has a job to do. So many people could have done it. Everyone's a suspect, of course. Even that Jung Bahadur, sitting on the floor, cupping Chandan's head in his hands. The old man looks fixedly at Chandan. Roma thinks it must be bred in his bones to be loyal to a master, any master.

"Madam we will escort you to government guesthouse where you will stay under police guard," the inspector says.

CHAPTER 58

When the train to Calcutta leaves Siliguri, the platform and train station are hushed. It's still dark. At turns in the hills, the Darjeeling Mail looks like a worm with a blazing, smoking head boring through mud.

Recently, this country has been betrayed—by those same English who knighted Sir Naren Mitter—into two independent people. Hindus and Muslims. Indians and Pakistanis. Roma knows about Cyril Radcliffe, a hapless political appointee, an entire stranger to India, no doubt overwhelmed, befuddled, who's drawn a line—wobbling? firm? who knows?—across India. He was told to create a new Hindu-ish India and a Muslim-ish Pakistan. So he's made the inept surgical cut that's bloodied what used to be thought of as India. Like, a cut through a Hindu latrine and a Muslim *dargah*, half of each on one side. The pen is mightier than the sword, after all. There are parallels, too: Chandan, butchered like a pig by an unknown blade; the country ripped like old cloth down its middle; her own botcheries of hope.

She has trunk called Mashimoni and Harish that she's coming to Calcutta. Harish said she shouldn't be traveling alone. She tells him there's no time for waiting. It's true and also a lie. Enough asking. She will just get to the house and everything will be fine. On her end, she wants to make the cut between past and present clean like a precise butcher's expert knife navigating, honoring, the membrane between skin, muscle, and organ. Nothing should bleed into another thing. Yes, everything must be separated purposefully. People die. Other people have to live. Go on.

Didn't she, after Roderick? Did she think of him after the dreams where he haunted, pursued her? No. She didn't. She buried him. Unless he drowned. How can a body just disappear? Or just stop breathing? Well, it seems it can, no use going on about it. She must reach Calcutta, must get home. She must prove herself again.

She's heard, of course, of the troubles in Calcutta. Independence came only a few days ago—August 15. Since then the old ancestral hatreds of Hindus and Muslims have become wildfires. Purges. Savagery. Killing, looting. Once family, community, neighbors, even lovers and kin, now bloody-minded killers, sniffing out the enemy: that one's a Hindu, this one's a Muslim. Mostly. But all this isn't new, of course. Wherever humans go, whatever they do, people kill and die. Live and let die.

She hasn't had a drink in days. She's leaving behind all of that with her time in Darjeeling.

As the train nears Calcutta, passengers get on and off at other stations babbling about terrible trouble in the northwest, in Delhi, Lahore, Amritsar; even in Calcutta. India and Pakistan have been born. The strange freedom birthed by the great Radcliffe guillotine. There are terrible rumors. Corpses the only passengers on incoming trains. No survivors. Death in cul de sacs, at lands' end. Ancestral hatreds have always bubbled, it seems, just beneath illusory comforts, foolish loves.

But Roma doesn't pay any mind. Calcutta is different. Calcutta is, whatever else it is, civilization.

Besides, she has nowhere else to go.

The train is approaching Howrah Junction. Just outside the station it slows down. She looks out. Up ahead she hears bogies uncoupling and coupling, tracks shifting. Clanging and grating. This is normal. At last. Just normal things. Normal sounds. She feels hope spill out as she looks out at that special Calcutta sunset sky splashed with pink, mauve, and yellow on a late summer day.

She feels elated, she feels weak, she feels free, and sentimental. Let's celebrate independence together—she mutters—you and I, my country. Butchered, betrayed, you have survived, whatever you had to let go. I will also survive, just you wait.

I'm sorry, Chandan. Goodbye, Chandan. I wish we'd been given a bit more time, my dear.

There's a sound like chanting or droning, even buzzing, coming from a distance. She can't quite place it. The bogies must now be retracked, because the train begins a slow creep forward. The sound can still be heard over axles grinding on slow moving wheels. It can't be mistaken for the general hum and din of the city. It is something else.

The train struggles into the station. Empty, but it feels as though it has been emptied suddenly, as if prepared in haste for impromptu theater. When the train reaches the covered platform, the sudden extinction of sunlight induces momentary blindness.

When the train finally screams to a stop, Roma sticks her head out her

window, looking for a coolie. Surprisingly, no horde instantly surges toward her. No one. The platform is lit only here and there by a sole, erratic bulb. The rest is shadow.

She steps off the compartment and walks a few paces. She sees a pile of what looks like abandoned luggage—sacks, bundles—around a pillar, and despairs. Is there a coolie strike then? It's too hazy to see properly. She feels deeply aggrieved. Is this how independence, hers included, is to be launched? What will she do now? Her two suitcases contain all her worldly possessions and they're too heavy for her to carry. She must find a coolie.

She walks, sourly but doggedly, sore and stiff from hours of traveling, toward the pile near the pillar. As she gets closer she smells a sharp, rancid stench. She goes on, covering her mouth and nose with a handkerchief. Stations are places for squatters, for the poor. So many have been dispossessed. Closer, she makes out some figures on the platform. All sleeping, it seems. Flies buzz around them.

Flies. Black flies, clouds of them, darting about. Why are there so many flies? She feels sad; a sad welcome back to the city. The great recent upheavals have damaged Calcutta. Riots. Refugees. Filthy streets and sewage. Now she has to swat the flies away from her face as she gets closer to the pile. She stumbles over something. Something small. She looks down.

It's a hand. Possibly a woman's. Chopped off at the wrist, fingers cactused, clawing inward as if something has been ripped out of them. The stench is much stronger. She sees dark, reddish splashes pulsating with black flies. Dark smears on the pillar. Around the pillar, bodies. A foot with a sock but no shoe. A head rolled a little away from the heap. A child's head. A face with its eyes gouged out. A woman—young, longhaired—staring wide-eyes at the ceiling. Her breasts are gone.

She only looks back once as she runs. When she looks back she sees dark footprints. Someone is following her. No, those are the prints of her own bloodied sandals. She stumbles, falls. She gets up, runs again. She doesn't look at the ground anymore. The distant chanting is growing clearer.

Later she will hear at least ten thousand people died that night in the city.

Snaking in and out of alleys, corners and shadows. Looking for safety. She keeps thinking she hears many feet stomping behind her. She doesn't know if they're echoes of her own or killers or prey. She tries to race ahead of her feet thudding clumsily in absurd, thin strapped sandals. Her vision dims every other second from sweat pouring into her eyes. She hears her own muffled, regular gasping and hiccupping as she tries to speed up, her eyes torqueing around her as she does. A new, desperate screech of metal against metal. A train has just pulled into a platform a few tracks away. The train's nose nuzzles into the grooved end of its journey. The engine sighs once, loud, harshly. She hesitates. Even stops. People might spill out of that train in seconds. There might be company, safety in numbers.

No one leaves the train.

Only a voice, maybe voices, rises in a keening, broken moan, like a million flies buzzing. A more guttural chanting.

She's reached a battleground, not civilization. On this day in 1947 the city is no more. There's only a very big field of carnage. An epic battle, an endless hunt, souls rising in flames from the slaughterhouse below. This much she gathers from the few skulking wraiths she runs into just outside Howrah Station. Everyone's running, looking for hiding places. As they stumble and scurry they scream at her, into the air, up to the sky, anywhere anyone will listen.

"Hide, hide, or they'll kill you . . . !"

"They" doesn't need to be counted or named. They are uncountable. A riot is in full swing. Hindus and Muslims are butchering one another. Like forever. Like the last decade. The last century. The last hundred years. The last thousand years.

She doesn't know how to get to Alipore, or where to go, or how to hide. She decides to try to follow the Ganges, the city's fluid spine. The arches of Howrah Bridge across the Ganges appear in the murky twilight like eyes from heaven looking at the ripped, bleeding city. Roma doesn't know if she's going fast or slow, if she's traveling toward safety or death. An invisible, furious beast lollops behind her. At one point a truck full of men brandishing swords and large knives rattle past. They shout: "Let's show you how to cut!" The cut they mean is the Partition of India, Radcliffe's carving knife serving up two halves of a country to its people. The "you" the men address, abstractly, are whatever enemy history and the empire have chosen for them, either Hindus or Muslims. She does her best to flatten herself against the transoms of the bridge's arches. Clamps her hand over her own mouth, just in case. The truck passes.

The growingly inky evening comes alive with pistils of distant flares as hate blooms. With every few yards of distance she covers, a long death rattle comes from the city, above the rumble and hissing of traffic, and the stomping and howling seemingly always just around a corner. She sees again, now closer and taller, flames licking the corners of the mottled sky. The homeless wind smells of burning flesh and fear.

Sometimes waves of people come rushing from other directions. Where are they going? Do they think they can just leave the city? A man, his face slicked with blood, shouts at her as they run past. "Don't go that way, lady . . . nothing but dying there, everything burning . . . they're cutting, don't go . . ." She lurches on. Where else will she go?

And then she's completely lost. Hopelessly lost. She's never seen this part of the city. The Mitters would never come to dismal, poor areas like this. The alleys are narrow, filthy. The gutters overflow with sewage. No streetlights. She's most afraid of stumbling on a body again. Dead or dying. Not far away, she can hear voices that sound like women and children. Whoops mixed in. Loud, angry curses. Sounds of hitting, of things being hit. Sounds without sense. She turns half-blindly into another, narrower lane, but suddenly its far end lights up with a bleary, blurry orange glow that becomes jiggling, leaping points of light. Torches approach. They come so fast that there isn't time to turn back. She tumbles into a gutter between two shanties live with a thick, flowing stream. The stench nearly makes her pass out. She squats neck deep in the flow.

The torch-carrying mob thunders past, screeching curses, promising slaughter. Her breath snags on her ragged sobs. For minutes she can't move though she knows she might pass out soon. Her hands shake and her legs threaten to fold but somehow she pulls herself out of the gutter. She lands like a gasping fish on the alley's slippery mud.

The next thing she can remember is stumbling onto a small city square with light from a single tall streetlamp. It's a square in a neighborhood of crisscrossing lanes. Three- or four-story houses stand around it. In the center a spreading tree. Patchy grass growing around it. An ornate metal fence barrier surrounding the trees, the grass. Common enough in the city: a flash of longing for the village, a little tenderness for a little patch of grass. The scene prints on her brain like a frame of a movie. The circular barrier has tall vertical spikes. A variety of body parts crown the spikes. Heads. One seems to be grinning. Maybe a grimace. It's a man's face, small and dark, the eyes wide and interested. Her eyes refuse to leave his face. Almost about to speak. Almost curious. Almost intrigued.

One of the houses surrounding the little square is in flames. On the top floor, shadows dance across the brilliantly throbbing windowpanes. The windows glow like yellow pearls. As the upper floor begins to explode and scatter, the screams become shriller. Then a motley crew of people like a convoy of ants burst out of the house. Toward her.

Again, more frames of a movie. She says to herself, so this is how it ends. Not fair.

But it's a free country now. Free to die. Free to kill. No more white masters. No more patriots. Just killing and dying.

The mob issuing from the house sees her. It makes a sound that cannot be described. Machetes, knives, and swords strike up a new dance, flash.

Rajani.

Roderick.

A car swerves into the square out of one of the dark lanes. The headlights flash once on the crowd—now a tableau in a frame—and then pick out their shapes, outlines. The mob cheers louder, now only a few yards away. The car screeches forward and swerves left between the mob and Roma. A door opens. A hand reaches out. Grasps her arm. She gives in. As she falls into the darkness inside, the door closes and the car begins to drive away.

CHAPTER 59

The man sitting next to her in the back says his name is Arindam Biswas. He was racing home to escape the frenzy on the streets, he says. His driver's face is invisible to Roma and he makes no motion at all. Biswas seems to be saying something. The driver may be watching her through the rearview mirror but she can't see it. Esplanade is roaring past her, some helpless torn thing

trailing behind as they hurtle on. Now it's almost dawn. At this hour you can send a taxi through the empty streets like a straight arrow through soft flesh.

She shakes her head to keep herself from falling asleep.

Biswas says he saw her and knew what was about to happen. "I'm happy to have risked my own life to save you, Miss . . . Mrs . . . ?"

Roma has no idea what the man is talking about. She doesn't in fact know what he just asked her. She did hear his name, but hasn't really heard anything since. She still sees the torches, though. Hears the feet. The yells. The burning building. The man called Arindam Biswas gives her something to drink. She sips it—it's whiskey. Its heat sears her parched, raw throat, and travels like a benediction through her. She shakes her head when he offers her more.

The car takes them to the Grand Hotel in Chowringhee. This part of the city is still fairly firmly under British and police control and should be relatively safe, Arindam Biswas explains. In the lobby there are a few Indian and mostly white people standing about, morosely sipping drinks, cigarettes and cigar smoke turning the air inside into a pale imitation of the smoky miasma outside in the streets. Roma struggles to walk and Arindam steadies her, holding her by the arm.

"Madam, what shall I call you?" He asks her again as he leads her through the grand lobby—it reminds Roma of Mitter Mansion, though this is larger—past ghostly men and women standing or sitting and smoking on the lounge sofas and not talking or even looking at anything, and up the spiral staircase to the upper floors. Uniformed and turbaned bearers part aside as they go, as if they too are voiceless phantoms.

Again, Arindam prods her: "Your name, madam?"

Some instinct, some dread makes Roma say, "My name is Mrs. Dutt. Reba Dutt." She herself doesn't know why she lies. Arindam Biswas seems like an average, regular man. And he's Bengali, like her. A middle- or upper middle-class English-speaking Bengali man. She couldn't be in safer hands. And this is the Grand Hotel after all. And this is Calcutta. What are those words she carried with her on the train to Calcutta, and even partway into Howrah Station? Calcutta. Civilization.

Yes. She will be safe in Calcutta, in the Grand Hotel especially. There are many people here, people who are also clinging to the hotel like ants to a spar floating in a flood. Nowhere to go now but forward.

Still, she makes up the name and glimpses—as has become a habit very quickly—momentarily a whole other person, a whole other past and life for this Reba Dutt who doesn't exist. Ideas, thoughts, keep flashing into view like scenes from the bioscope. Words are gone at the moment. This is a relief, actually; she doesn't want to talk.

They are in a room now. The room is cool and dark, and outside sound is mostly inaudible. The air conditioner is humming genteelly. Biswas walks to a gramophone radio on a console and switches it on. Band music fills the room.

He lowers the volume. Now it's like a stream rippling through rocks. He tells her to sit down, be comfortable. She sits. She looks around the room. There's a telephone in the corner. Solid, black, reassuring. She has to make the phone call. She will do it soon. Call Mashimoni at the mansion. But she can't move yet. Very tired. Very, very tired. She hasn't slept for a day and a night. Her clothes smell terrible. It's sewage. She gags once she registers that for herself. Gags and stumbles to the en-suite bathroom and throws up violently, for a long time. She turns on the shower and steps under the cold water with her clothes on. The water begins to wash her, her hair, her clothes, slowly warming up as it does, and she lets it get very hot. Steam is rising around her, out of the shower stall, into the bathroom, misting the mirror. She can see the mist spreading.

"Everything okay, madam?" Biswas asks outside. She has no desire to respond. She doesn't. Silence again outside. The running water drowns out any other sounds there are, and she stands under it for she doesn't know how long.

She steps out of the shower and finds a clean towel on the towel rack. She begins to take off her clothes, then remembers she has no change of clothes. So with the towel she dries her hair, pats her face, her arms, her torso, passing it up below the hem of her sari to reach her calves, her knees, as far as she can. She hesitates to lift the entire lower half of her sari, then does it and rubs hard at her thighs, between her legs, the part of her stomach under her navel. She wrings the sari she's wearing, squeezes moisture out of it, leaving a small pool on the floor. She leaves the bathroom as it is, vaporing, wet, water standing.

She sits down on the sofa near the telephone. She must make a call. She looks at the double bed with the coverlet neatly folded at the bottom. She wants to throw herself on it, right now, go to sleep. But first she has to make the call. It's very important.

Biswas comes near her, solicitous. "Madam can I get you something?"

She says simply, "A cup of tea, please."

"Nothing a little stronger?" Biswas asks. "Not a little brandy to keep you strong?"

She realizes within ten minutes of downing the brandy that she is sinking. And that Biswas is now sitting on the sofa next to her. The radio is playing some kind of jazz. She feels the edges of her vision blur. Her body blurs too; her contour begins to melt and roll down her sides. Arms start vanishing. Feet are dissolving too. It feels good, though, the unfamiliar warm, fuzzy feeling growing in the pit of her stomach as the clear amber liquid—and something else—still works its way down. She tries to swing her legs, feels them swim up to the surface of her senses, and laughs out loud. Biswas is suddenly much closer. His left arm has come up and lies on her shoulder.

At some point, while she giggles and blubbers about how much she loves music, because she loves the bioscope—that they have practically been her only school—she feels his head on her shoulder, as if seeking friendly comfort. Poor guy, she thinks fuzzily, it must be hard to be as ugly as he is. He might even be a little in love with her. She feels sorry for him.

Someone's singing contralto with the popular film music streaming out of the radio in the corner; at some point Biswas changed the station, obviously,

after hearing that she loves the bioscope, film music. She hears his voice pouring onto her neck in duet, his rough, smoke-scorched lips rasping on her skin.

He pulls her closer, hip to hip. She hears herself taking a long breath. The small room is lit by a single floor lamp, and everything around the halo of lamplight is fuzzy darkness. She likes that too. It makes her feel light and glamorous, like a bioscope heroine. Back-lighting. No words at all now; only a massive din in her head. In a far corner of her brain she hears an alarm bell ringing, but can't move fast enough. Actually she can't move at all, or so it would seem because the man—she can't remember his name now though she tries hard so she can call it out, shout out—grabs her by the arms, pins her down, and pushes himself upon her, half sitting, half lying. He pushes his tongue, his lips, his thing, into her mouth; she gags on his tumescent organ. His mouth and his hard stumpy thing choke her, cut off her voice. He tears at her blouse, ripping off the back hooks and fiddling frantically with her bra strap. She is flung back hard. She closes her eyes. Let it happen, she thinks, knowing it's a mindless, bottomless thought. She can see, hazily, the man's veined, red-rimmed eyes boring into that bottomlessness. She gasps when she feels him tearing into her and then tearing away inside her. Her pelvis fills with pain. He begins to give great, big thrusts, and a roar grows out of him.

After he rolls off, she doesn't know how much later, she finds she can move her legs though they are heavy, and stiff with pain. She raises herself, tries to stand. Despite her loathing, her fear, she slumps back on the man, though, because her legs give way as she tries to stand. He laughs, lying there limp and exposed, his pants down at his knees, his stubby, hairy thighs pushing up from them like huge worms. Something oozes out of her, between her legs and from her eyes. She closes her eyes. Falls asleep.

She has difficulty waking up to Biswas prodding her with a cup of tea. The pain between her legs and in her pelvis is duller. She can walk. She says she has to go to the bathroom first. She goes. Looking down at herself she finds she's wearing only a bra and a petticoat. *How many more times has he done it?* She touches herself after she sees the thin streamers of red on the white ceramic of the commode. Her fingers have semidried, pulpy blood on them. She tries to turn on the sink faucet and the effort of the torque makes her fall on the bathroom floor that's still wet. She lies there for minutes, or maybe more. This time Biswas doesn't come to the door and ask her if she's alright. She imagines the biscuit-colored skin forming on the tea in the cup and gags. She throws up on the wet, sticky tiles. After voiding her stomach of the sour, glutinous pulp in it, she crawls back into the room, toward the bed, pulls herself up on it and falls in. After that, again, she doesn't remember.

Only in the car later, wherever it's now taking her, she tries to clench her core muscles with great resolve, as someone might who fears limbs, skin, eyes, and mouth ungluing, separating, under the swirling, rushing waters of heavy-lidded self-loathing. She glimpses the tear in the universe gaping beyond

this moment, but she can't move or speak very well.

The car stops in a locality she doesn't know. There are many ramshackle buildings leaning on each other, most of their windows showing a woman or two standing or leaning out. She can see better now. The women seem to be dressed colorfully. There are a lot of muddier colors of neglect and decay splotching the brackish outer walls of the houses, some with cracks traveling up several stories from foundations. She's taken inside one of the houses by Biswas and the driver. She is trembling and can't place her steps one after the other, so they semihoist her by her arms through the door, which opens into a passageway with several doors lining both sides. The passageway is narrow and painted a jarring blue, but there's light showing faintly above suggesting a more open space upstairs. She's taken upstairs and lowered onto a bed. Her eye falls on a fat woman sitting on a low cot at the end of the room, smoking a cigarette. The woman says nothing, doesn't move. A tray is brought in by another, younger woman. She sets it down on a coffee table in the middle of the room, between the bed and the cot. The young woman leaves. There's a teapot, cups and a plate of food on the tray. Roma smells the aroma of fried, deep-spiced meat. Involuntarily her mouth waters and her stomach growls. The man called Biswas laughs. He brings her a serving of mutton cutlets on a small plate. She falls on the plate and starts to put the food inside her mouth.

The fat woman on the cot and Biswas watch her. Biswas eats cutlets and smokes and drinks tea at the same time. He gnaws upon the mutton bones and spits out gristle periodically. She can see his teeth now; they are spotted yellow brown and crooked. His searching, piggish eyes rarely leave her. He periodically purses his thin lips and rubs his nose, almost picking it. She sees that he has dirt-rimmed, yellowed fingernails.

Finally, he and the fat woman lean toward each other. They whisper. There seems to be some disagreement, and the woman speaks closer into his ear. His eyes still stay on Roma's face. Now she is lying in the bed, on her back again, her head turned slightly toward them. From this angle it is hard to see them well. *She just wants to sleep. Please. Things can change quickly.*

CHAPTER 60

It's a bleak winter. Harish searches for Rehana. He searches for his son. When the rioting started he began to collapse; had to pull himself together somehow. Rehana is easy prey. Men are going from house to house, neighborhood to neighborhood, picking, pulling out women who don't seem to have menfolk around them, sometimes even those who do. Ordinary folk can't do anything. The men are armed, often drunk or drugged, in the mood for carnage. Then the women don't come back. People go report to the authorities. India and Pakistan are trying to locate missing women and restore them to their families or at least to their countries. There will even be an act passed for this soon: the

Abducted Persons Recovery and Restoration Act. But hundreds of thousands of women are missing.

In every rescue camp in Delhi and Lahore there are thousands of women, they say. Some have babies. Newborns. Or they are pregnant. Their families are contacted but they won't take them back because they are ruined. Because they are carrying the fruits of the enemy's seed. Because they have been raped by Satan and borne his children. Satan's name is Muhammad, and also Ram. Et cetera.

These are the unlucky ones. Survivors. Many of them sit like stones in one place. They don't eat. They don't look at people in front of them. Around them. They don't cry. They don't speak. Some of them hold or sit near babies they don't look at, whom they won't feed, who have to be fed sugar water by small, harassed groups of volunteers who are doing what they can. Which is not enough. The Abducted Persons Act has created living ghosts. Ghosts with babies. Mother India.

Harish goes from camp to camp. Even travels up to the northern camps. Delhi. Rawalpindi. Multan. Nothing. He tries to get permission to enter Pakistan, which is impossible.

In the camps there are also women who cry, who beg to be allowed to go back, to be sent back. Who rage and hurl abuse and sometimes things at volunteers, at the officers and police who patrol the camps. "Who told you to bring us back?" They scream. "Who are you to tell us where to go? We have children on the other side!" They mean the other side of the India-Pakistan border. The new border. The Radcliffe line. They ask why they've been brought back. "Who's going to take me back now?" They shout. "You think my husband wants me back, soiled? What's left in me now?"

And then there are those who are simply missing. Door to door searches have failed to yield them up on either side of the border. Some have died on trains. Some are probably rotting at their doorsteps with no one in the house beyond. Some are lying on the beds of rivers, ponds, wells. These are the lucky ones.

Of course he goes first to the old kotha. Pyari Bai doesn't live there anymore. "Where are they?" He asks beseechingly. "Where is Rehana? Please, I just want to make sure she's alright. This is a dangerous time for everyone, especially for women."

"Hai hai sahib," one of the women says, "You think we don't know that times are dangerous? It's just that for us, for women like us, times have always been dangerous, they'll always be dangerous. So we aren't afraid."

But her companion spits.

The companion is wearing an angrakha-ghagra twice her size and incongruous in daytime. Her hair is a tired, angry red though it is obvious that under the henna dye she must be close to white haired. Maybe once she was beautiful, sought after, well rewarded. Now her face is cracked and darkened with age and her nearly pebble glass spectacles sit crookedly over eyes trampled by birds' feet. Her lips and mouth cave inward over her few remaining teeth.

She spits, then trundles forward and pushes her face right into Harish's.

"Truth is, it's only women like us who are truly safe now, Mitter Sahib. What's happening to all those good womenfolk out there is only what's been happening to us most of our lives. Just that we can deal with it, we have lived all our lives with you vultures around. You see?" Her voice is discordantly booming.

Harish rushes out of the house, runs into others nearby.

Nothing is discovered. No one knows where mother and daughter and baby went. Or they aren't telling. They won't tell. It's the little bit of satisfaction they can get out of their lifelong puppeteers. Look who's crying now, they titter. Look who's dancing at the end of the string now.

In other houses too, no one knows. So many women are being brought, they say. What's the harm if a few have left? Replacements easily available. Peals of laughter drive Harish and other men on similar quests out of the houses.

And Roma never arrives. Prem sends men out on a search. "Go to Howrah Station," she instructs. "Make especially extensive inquiries there. She was supposed to have come by the Darjeeling Mail." Someone must know something.

In the top drawer of her writing desk is a photo of the three children when they were going to school. Her three children. She firmly believes they are hers. Of the three, Harish was probably the least waited upon by the household because she always worried more for the other two, especially for Roma. Though Harish went through his fervently nationalist phase before ten, and heads may have got bumps during that time, there was never any question that he adored Roderick. Though he was also jealous of him. These things can and do coexist.

Why couldn't Muslims and Hindus have coexisted in independent India? In spite of fallings out and jealousies and even rages, why couldn't they? There were so many villages, so many *parganahs* and towns where they had lived side by side, peacefully, for hundreds of years. What happened to drive them at each other's throats? Why did millions of people lose faith in each other, cut the throats of neighbors, publicly rape and mutilate the women they'd once called mother, sister, or daughter? Prem cannot fathom an answer.

The British dealt their hand well. And not just in the last few years leading up to independence. For decades, maybe centuries, they played the gadfly, the ambassadors of hate. Set this Hindu Raja at that Muslim Nawab. Made Muslims in general believe that the Hindu majority was waiting to fall on them as soon as the British left. Made Hindus believe that Muslims were just biding their time to chop off their heads, dishonor their women, and pollute their bloodlines. Stroked and vitiated the monstrous ego of Muhammad Ali Jinnah, the Moses of the Muslim League. Dragged Gandhi around at the end of the rope of Round Table Conferences. A system of divide and conquer. Devil's dice. Till the end.

She thinks these things and also of her own husband. For thirty years she's watched that man live off the leavings of the British. Flatter them, extoll them, seek their praise. Turn his back on his country, his people, his duties to his society. The oration he was giving the night of her last annual ball, the night Roderick probably burned to death, returns to her. Nattered on and on about

the idea of the natural slave and the natural aristocrat. About the 'peon.' Sir Naren was obviously not a peon, he would have you understand. And for the first few years of her marriage she had believed. Though she'd learned quickly every pathetic weakness of his nature, every calculating *blandeur* in his eyes, she'd given him the benefit of her doubt.

Inequality was nature's way, society's way. He'd said that again and again, throughout the marriage, and she hadn't taken very long to realize that he was a pompous, selfish and cowardly man saying what suited him best to say and even think. Could she go as far as to suspect that maybe he'd always preferred Roderick to Harish because Roderick was half English? The superior sort of mankind, as he used to intone? She shouldn't—she has to pull herself back from that pit.

Harish, she assumes, goes looking for Roma. When he comes home, sometimes after days at a time, she meets him at the dinner table and wants to touch his head, stroke his hair. His face is drawn. He's lost a great deal of weight. She wants to ask him what he knows, what's happening out there. Sometimes he says a few words. Mostly he eats with his head low over his plate, saying nothing. Asking for nothing. Not even for salt.

Poor boy, Prem thinks. My poor boy. I've lost two children and he's lost the only brother and sister he ever had. What comfort is there for him? What can she say or do? She, who cannot herself leave the house because of what's happening outside. And because she's always dazed. She sometimes wants to tell Sir Naren what's happening. She needs someone to talk to, but there's no one to unburden herself to.

Where is Roma? What might be happening to her? She will not let herself ask questions like whether she's dead or alive. She just will not go to that place. Harish has told her that the police are of little use. How many cases will they solve? How many women will they look for? Already there are house to house searches and in most of them the police face angry families, distraught relatives and questions with answers no one can remember.

After dinner he always comes around to kiss her cheek—he's always been an affectionate son—and she doesn't ask the question dunning her. He knows that. He says, "Not yet, Mother. I'll let you know."

He looks for his Didi too, of course. Since the night she didn't arrive his heart has been ripped apart between two geographies of love. And a third. The child he's never seen. He regrets bitterly every waking moment that he turned them loose, that he let Rehana go, because he was a coward. He wonders what would have happened had he had that courage. What was the worst that could have happened? His parents would have disinherited him? He would have been asked to leave? His child would have grown up disowned?

Or maybe none of that would have happened. It's hard for him to imagine being banished by his mother, especially. His mother who had once taken in his father's half-English son. He knows she had loved Roderick truly, dearly. Would it have made that much difference to her that her grandchild's mother was Muslim? Surely his mother had always revealed far greater magnanimity that his father? His father and she had always crossed swords on human worth, on

charity, on generosity. Why had he thought that such a mother, such a woman, would have closed her door on a Muslim girl and her own grandchild? Why had he not trusted her? Not given her more credit for who she truly was?

She is mostly semiconscious these days. Sometimes her speech slurs; sometimes she can't be woken from sleep. Maybe it's better that way, at least for now.

He visits his father in his room every night he's home. He wants to be a good son. His father can't speak. He can only move his head slightly in either direction. His wide, staring eyes alone follow someone moving in the room, someone coming, someone leaving. He feels very sorry for his father. The night Roderick's indubitable disappearance was confirmed, his father had his third massive stroke. He has not left his bed since then. The doctors think it is not likely he ever will.

"How are you today, Papa?" Harish asks dutifully each time he visits. Though his father's eyes are blank, still, and clouded, he thinks his father can understand and something makes him think his father wants to ask him something. It's a good thing he can't; there are few answers.

Is he himself a coward? He wonders. Everyone knew Roderick was a hero. Because Roderick was a hero. And he died being a hero. The death of a hero. And what has he, Harish, done? Who has he been? What has he been? Sengupta now almost entirely runs the company, and in fact acts more and more everyday as if he owns it. Harish doesn't doubt that with Sengupta's party connections— of course Sengupta is now a member of the Congress Party and of the West Bengal Chief Minister Prafulla Chandra Ghosh's inner circle—he will no doubt facilitate the nationalization of the Mitter family businesses, especially given the state government's failure to create new industries.

Cassius, Harish calls him privately. Lean, gaunt and serpentine, Sengupta occasionally meets with him to have him sign 'important papers.' Harish has taken to signing the papers without reading them. He doesn't have the strength to envision the coming age. He thinks sometimes of the time when as a younger man he thought his father stood in the way of progress. Now, though only barely thirty, he sometimes thinks he stands where his father may have feared standing. He thinks; he cannot know. His father will not be able to talk about this, or about anything else. Himself, he almost longs for the brutal efficiency of the British: the railways, the prisons, the postal system, the army, law and order. He remembers almost with disbelief and longing the punctuality of trains in his youth. His time, his father's time, was the time of the British, probably. That's why he feels regressed and synchronized with that age, when time comported itself decently, when the British ran the railways like stern gods, no matter if in the avatar of the drunken Irish or Anglo-Indian engine driver. Now, time is a barbarian like the whistling, loutish youth of the neighborhood.

Even Alipore has become an extension of the neighboring dockyards of Kidderpore and its colorful population of sailors, drunks, smugglers, thieves, whores and pimps. Every time he leaves the mansion now in one of the family cars—though the Rolls Royce has been sold by Sengupta who invoked budget shortfalls in the business accounts as the reason for this—he sees all this. He remembers his childhood and youth when the idea of sharing the broad main

streets with such people would have been risible to men like his father.

Some of his schoolmates have switched gears to the new age and are thriving. They've become Congress allies and lackeys. They are being suitably rewarded for this allegiance. An old habit of bowing to a master: once British, now Indian. Somehow, he knows he won't be able to fall in the same line and do as they're doing. Oddly, now the past pulls him, drags at him too hard for it. He thinks of the child he never saw. He doesn't know if the child is still alive. He doesn't know if he had a son or a daughter.

What a time that was. Him and Jaanu. Not a thing standing between them, not one serpent in that garden of love. Him drowning in all she brought with her name, her music, her beauty, and her daily tributes of imagination, and she also, she would say, drowning in a lover not hardened and tainted by habitual duplicity and debauchery. What a spring. What hope. She'd begun singing for the bioscope. So happy that made her. And him, seeing how happy she was though he was still cautious, of little faith, worrying for her well-being, worrying about his masquerade. Such a future they might have had. A new empire, even. Of poetry and vision, not concrete and steel. He let it all slip through his hands because he was so afraid. He was mortally afraid. He was afraid of being seen as who he really was. Who he remains. A poet, not a merchant. Not an aeronaut but an Argonaut.

Surely?

He goes out in the evenings. Drinks at the clubs, slumps at cabarets. Comes home so drunk sometimes that the driver has to carry him in, practically. He hates meeting his mother's eyes, themselves reddened and half-open, the next morning.

Prem has finally touched rock bottom. She tried to believe Harish goes out in the hope that he might see Roma one night. See her as what they both fear Roma may now be. Unless she's dead.

Harish goes to the clubs, to the nightclubs and the cabarets not after hope. He goes because he cannot hope, think, anticipate any longer. He's convinced that the worst has happened. He's convinced that all he's doing is counting down to the time when he will no longer be able to pay to get into the expensive clubs for once-rich boys like him. He goes because he just wants to drink, to be left alone.

CHAPTER 61

Late one night a car returning from a film premier collides head on with a freight lorry loaded with steel beams and masonry on Circular Road in central Calcutta. The lorry driver who was drunk dies instantly. In the car, Jagat Pandey's driver dies instantly too. The car engine explodes. Jagat Pandey is rushed to the hospital and dies early the next morning. He's badly burnt and his heart fails.

Harish goes to pay his respects. Jagat Pandey's body lies in the front draw-ing room in the Theatre Roadhouse. Lovely, patient Damayanti—Jagat's be-loved Madam Prudence Cooper—remains gazing upward into the floodlit heaven that is hers forever like a merciful angel praying for Jagat Pandey's soul. Jagat Pandey lies on a white pallet, on a marble floor, with another white sheet covering it, tuberoses shushing and garnishing a violent death, white cotton-wool pads in his nostrils and ears detaining the soul till it can leave the body with appropriate fanfare at the cremation grounds on the banks of the Ganges in Calcutta.

Prem reads in the obituary section of *The Statesman* the next day of "the tragic, accidental passing of the eminent filmmaker and true patriot Honorable J. Pandey, a genius of the moving image who eschewed politics as usual and politicians, but made his bioscope art the vehicle of his deepest, purest love for India and Indians." He began his film career, it is stated, as an assistant director to Jamshedji Framji Heeravala, whose first sensational hit *Nala Damayanti* (1921) changed the course of Indian bioscope. A smallish grainy picture in a longer article about Pandey Sahib shows eminent actors, actresses and film personalities of the day keeping wake around his mortal remains. All Prem can see is a body on a white sheet on a white marble floor, the pallid faces of wake-keepers, a vague impression of tufts of cotton wool plugged into the nostrils and ears of the dear departed so that soul and body are not untimely and irretrievably partitioned.

She feels sad that one of the makers of *Nala Damayanti* has died, and un-timely. She suddenly remembers as though it were yesterday the excitement she felt, those twenty-odd years ago, when she went to see that film. Roma had gone with her. She was six or seven. On the way back Roma had lectured her Mashimoni about wifely duties and virtues.

If only everything could be done over again. If only Kanan hadn't married the Kuleen Horse. If she herself hadn't been in a great hurry to marry and leave her father's house, thinking that leaving the village behind was her only way to survive. If, if. . . . If Roderick hadn't died. If Lilian hadn't come back for him. Traveling back in time past is a lonely, painful journey, but Prem can't not linger in it a little. There's so little left to look forward to.

When she and Kanan had made up this little fairytale about their two names she'd believed in a garden where love would grow and bloom forever. Well, she wasn't a very good gardener then—she let many sweet things die—but later she did try to water and shade the little lives that came out of the fairytale, didn't she?

I tried.

She knows that Sengupta is stealing the business away from under their noses day by day. And sometimes she thinks she should do something about it. Harish has clearly lost all interest in the business, and—sometimes her heart twists to think—perhaps in life. And he's lost most of the people dearest to him. And why he's never found a woman to love or marry, she can't understand. And how Sir Naren never understood his little son's heart, never saw how he hurt that boy by openly preferring his older son, whom the boy still idolized.

And how Lilian changed, so completely changed, because of history and the Raj and who knows what else. Maybe just time.

And, above all, how she never replied when they telegrammed her about Roderick's disappearance. How could she do that? *What kind of mother . . . ?* Is she even alive? Prem certainly doesn't expect ever to know.

And then, what is left of the village? After Saroj came away to Calcutta, who took charge of the farm and the property? Does the old head Munshi still do it? Is he still alive?

And what grief her mother kept buried in her heart for a lifetime. The short blade did its work as long as it could, then the blade of relentless guilt and grief cut her loose from the world, and then from herself; set her floating into delirium and then oblivion. She never came back. Maybe she'd always wanted just that, to unmoor and uncouple. And maybe forcing herself to stay moored to an intolerable consciousness was her only way of loving the daughter she didn't want, until she simply couldn't any longer.

And maybe that's all there is. Beyond the promises, and the struggles and the heartbreaks and little and big lies, everyone is just doing what they can, what they're best at. Maybe that's the best everyone can do.

And maybe so has she, Lady Premlata Mitter.

I tried; I really tried.

CHAPTER 62

Harish is having his morning coffee in the library, where he now sits most of the day, like Sir Naren once did. He's not sure how he'll spend the rest of the day. He has nothing to do. He generally avoids crowds now, even where he doesn't know anyone. He has no need to go to the company office on Rawdon Street. Rather, the office has no need for him to come. The Alipore horse races are on, but he is not a betting man, and in any case he has ridiculously little money these days. Doesn't feel like making a pathetic sod of himself with the loaded fat cats of his acquaintance. Friends have vanished with money. Also, in the last years he mostly let his life revolve around his family, his parents, his siblings, and later Rehana. So where does he go?

A note is brought in to him. It was delivered by hand, he's told. The bearer, who left immediately, said he'd not been asked to stay for a response. That the sahib would know what to do.

Inside, Harish reads a brief message in unsteady Hindi calligraphy.

"Mitter Sahib, your son and his mother are leaving for *Umricah* with a white man. She doesn't know I'm sending you this letter. Maybe you can see your son one last time if you make haste."

Harish doesn't answer his mother's anxious questions as he tears out of the library, then the house, and summons the driver to take him to the address given at the bottom of that short note. The driver immediately puts the last

remaining car—the Baby Austin—in gear. He stops, blinks and says, "Sahib, not enough petrol in tank." Harish pushes him aside and gets in the driving seat himself. He grinds the ignition key, presses the gas pedal as hard as he can. The great beast of an automobile roars, shudders, and perishes in little, miserable spurts. The gas gauge is in fact empty. Even had Harish had the heart to abuse the driver for his carelessness and negligence in not having the gas tank filled the night before, he knows it is no use. The driver doesn't get enough money in advance to keep the car filled with petrol at all times. Nowadays he's generally given a small sum at the week's beginning and told to manage with it till the end. It's Saturday. The driver has run out of money to buy petrol.

Harish turns out his own pockets, which are empty. He pulls out his wallet and fishes in it, his hands shaking. He has no money. Nothing. He remembers now that his mother asked him for some money a few days ago for household expenses. Since then he's neither needed his wallet, nor used it.

"Go to madam," he tells the driver, "and tell her to send me cash to buy petrol. Tell her it's urgent." The driver runs off into the house. Harish lowers his head on the steering wheel and sits unmoving. The driver returns in about two minutes but he only brings a few paltry notes. They won't be enough. "Madam says this is all there is in the house right now, sahib," he says ruefully.

"Sukhdev Singh, can you lend me some money?" Harish asks the driver.

In shock, the driver withdraws a few bills from his pocket and slowly hands them over to his master. "No, not to me, just go get some petrol to fill the tank and hurry up and then drive me out," Harish says, pushing the bills back toward Sukhdev Singh and turning him around physically toward the gate, and Sukhdev Singh begins walking.

With the petrol Sukhdev Singh buys the car makes good speed. Saturday traffic is light in the mornings. Harish finds himself in this neighborhood called the Bow Barracks, a part of the city he's never been to. The houses here are sturdy and tall, mostly old-fashioned squat structures, painted a fading red on the outside, with dark-green wood-shuttered windows. As the car crawls forward and Harish looks for the house number he sees a mostly sleepy, placid neighborhood, with life stirring faintly. A few bakery type of shops are brewing strong milky tea, and a vendor or milkman cycles past the car ringing the bell merrily and loudly. A few children are playing cricket on the roads, but adults are generally invisible. Washing hangs down almost to the first floors from the balconies of higher stories, mostly European clothes dancing merry jigs in the mellow morning sun. Finally, Harish's eye falls on the number: 12051. The car screeches to a halt though it was traveling slowly, Harish's exclamation causing Sukhdev Singh to hit the brakes hard. Harish gets out of the car.

He's still chubby, and jumping up two steps at a time makes him breathe stertorously, sweat quickly running in rivulets down his temples and face. The address is Flat 43, 12051 Henry Street. When he rings the bell at the door of Flat 43 he feels dizzy, his heart and lungs hurting as if in a brawl with his breath. He thinks he will black out, but this only frightens him enough to stay conscious because otherwise he will miss Rehana and the baby and so lose them for the rest of his life. He presses down hard on the doorbell with the flat of

one hand and pounds on the door with the other hand balled into a fist.

The door opens and he nearly falls into the room. Pyari Bai stands before him, then moves out of his way to let him enter. His eyes try adjusting to the darkness of the room. All the windows are closed.

"Where are they?" he asks.

She doesn't say anything for a few seconds. Then, unexpectedly, she shouts, "You come now?"

He stares, bewildered. Their faces mirror anguish but he feels a surge of joy in himself. He will see Rehana. And he will see his son. And finally things will change. He will never ever let her go again. He will shoo away the American, maybe even pay him off. And he will make a very good father, an excellent father, smothering his son with all the love he has missed.

"You asked me to come, and I'm here. Where is she, Pyari Bai-ji?"

And again she says, but this time closer to a whisper, and not as a screaming question, "You come now." Then she raises her face toward the ceiling and shrills, "She's gone! She has left! She didn't stay! They all went away." Covering her mouth with her shaking hands the old, heavyset woman doubles down and slowly slides against a wall till she reaches the floor.

"Bring her back! Oh! Bring her back, sahib! Bring my daughter back!" Her voice, rasping and yet clogged, breaks at each syllable; the words become long, straining howls.

Harish looks around the room. His eyes have now adjusted to the darkness and he sees a low divan, a few chairs, and a low table. He looks at the old woman. As if suddenly understanding what she said he rushes to her side, stoops, tries to lift her, help her off the floor. But she's too heavy, and he's too out of shape. So he sits down by the floor beside her and watches. He's too late. It's over, and he can only watch Rehana's old, wretched mother cry.

"Sahib, why did you let her go? Why didn't you stay? Why did you leave, run away, when she begged you to take her? Why, sahib? Is your heart made of stone?"

Yes, his heart must be made of stone. And the rest of him is turning to stone as well.

Just about an hour before he arrived—probably just as he got the car to run again with the petrol bought with the driver's money—Rehana, the baby, and her new American husband walked out the door, Pyari Bai says, though she threw herself at her daughter's feet and begged her not to leave.

"Umrican soldier, sahib. Took my daughter and the boy, promised to care for the boy like his own. But wouldn't take me. Said Umricah won't let me come."

"And Rehana?"

"I asked her how she could leave, her country, her mother, her whole world, and she just said, 'What's here for me, Mother? You?' "

And so his great love affair has finally ended. Harish watches Pyari Bai cry. Sometimes she looks up at him and begins to curse him anew. She says he's a murderer, a liar, an animal, a monster. She taunts his unmanliness, his spinelessness. She calls him a devil, a thief, an evil spirit. He wants her to do this. He wants to hear her say this is who he is. This is who he is. A coward, a

fool, and a beggar. Neither aeronaut nor Argonaut.

She says he hopes he and his family die and rot in hell, while worms eat their insides. Then they will know what it is to lose all hope. To take a miserable, ruined woman's only daughter away from her. To ruin her again, to condemn her to darkness for the rest of her days.

He listens, and hopes that yes, he at least should rot in hell. He wants this to happen. Not to his family. But to himself. All of it. More. All the curses against him and his kind stored up in the heart of this woman and others like her . . . he hopes they all come true. That his life be blighted as hers is.

When the flat door closes behind him, the sun seems to have traveled a good distance. The day outside has aged and is tilting into its decline. It's almost dark. An abandoned woman in Flat 43, 12051 Henry Street, Bow Barracks, Calcutta has cried nearly the day through. He has no comfort for her. She will cry for the rest of her days and sicken and die alone.

Standing right in the middle of the landing on the fourth floor of 12051 Henry Street, Harish looks around. The discolored, mud-streaked mosaic tiles have not been cleaned in a long time. There's litter all over the floor: crumpled paper, cigarette ends, dead leaves, green coconut shell fragments, some animal turd hardening in a corner. My son spent the first years of his life here, he thinks. He realizes now, suddenly, that he doesn't have a photo of the boy. He has no idea what the kid looks like.

There he cries—standing in that glum, lightless landing where the solitary, naked bulb at the end of a wire overhead is a dead eye watching his agony—for the first time since he arrived. He lowers his face into his hands and cries silently, his ample flesh contracting and expanding as he breathes, his body shaking from the violence of his sobs. The door of another flat opens onto the landing and loud voices spill out. One is a woman's voice, the other a man's.

"Two hours, that was the agreement, bitch! I paid good money for this, and you better shell out!"

"Let me go!" The woman screams at breaking pitch. "Let me go, you dirty bastard!"

The man lunges at her, missing her by inches. Harish watches dully. He wonders if this is what happens in the other flats here. If it used to happen in Flat 43. Where Rehana and his son lived.

"Come back!" The man roars. The light from the room illuminates him better than the woman who is half into the landing. He's wearing a sleeveless cotton vest. He's white. For no particular reason Harish looks at the man's feet. White feet, pale and craggy, gripping the mosaic that extends into the flat too. Unsteady, shifting, rebalancing. Feet that couldn't run far or fast.

She should run away now, Harish thinks. The man is obviously blotto. She should take this opportunity and run. She does take a step toward the stairs. He realizes now that she's as drunk as the man. She takes another small, uncertain step and then she falls. She falls like a palette of bricks, without restraint or pattern. She simply falls in a heap, and lies still for a second. Then she begins to try to skid away, her hands clawing at the filthy mosaic, her arms flailing like a drowning swimmer, her body like a snail attempting to hurry away from

harm. Harish wants to tell the man to stop, to let the woman be. He wants to help her off the dirty floor, down the steps, hail a taxi, put her in it. Before he can take a step, trying to fight off his fatigue, his lightheadedness and his grief—for this moment, this day, this life—the man comes out of the flat and lands upon the woman and begins to beat her. He beats her as if she were a thing. As if she were a door he's pummeling to be let in. He slaps her again and again around the face. He pulls her head up by the hair and then he slams it down onto the floor. Harish hears a cracking sound.

The woman isn't making any sounds anymore. Harish can only hear the thwacking sounds and the occasional flat-handed slap. And he inches forward, all of him shaking, his muscles refusing this unaccustomed task of bearing a large, crouching body, his heart thudding so hard he thinks it will suddenly shatter, throwing him back into the middle of the landing in a backward arc. But he talks to his heart, his muscles, his tendons, his nerves. "Hold on one moment longer. Just a little longer. Hold on!" And they do, they do go with him, and he travels with them toward where the man is still on the woman and he doesn't know how but he raises his right foot as high as he can and then with one decisive movement brings it down on the head of the man just as the man looks up for a split second and then he hears a sound of bone hitting something hard.

Then nothing. And then he sees, now that he's closer, that the man is holding a bottle in one hand, still, and he leans forward and snatches the bottle from the man and brings it down again on the man's head and hears a shattering sound but it's not the bottle because it's still whole when he brings it back up but there's blood on it.

Now back to the woman. His weak heart is thundering like wild horses galloping, but he can see that she's still moving slightly. He counsels and cheers every step his body allows him to take toward her. Counting. One, two, three, and she's only a few feet away from him. Amazingly, beginning to try to push herself up from the floor.

Are they the only people in the world, or at least in this building? The man on the floor behind him, and he and the woman?

Then he hears glass crunching.

Part 9:

Return to the Village, 1950

CHAPTER 63

"And this is where we made our brave plans for the new future."
Prem shows Roma the precise spot by the pond—it's still there, in thirty years very little has changed at the core of the village—where she and Kanan sat and worked out the future: their children marrying, and life and the century and the rest of civilization and time going on happily ever after.

A little distance behind them can be heard frequent slapping and exclamations. The young servant from Calcutta is experiencing country life for the first time.

"A nice place for dreams, Mashimoni."

The pondside is still what it was, though so much else has changed. The village hasn't quite decided what to do with independent modernity. Areas of it have eagerly adapted to new times and new ways—hopefully better times, better ways—and others have declined as yet. The railway station, some main roads, the post office, have acquired new beauties; a county hospital and a farm affairs bureau have recently cropped up. But the fields, orchards, local and neighborhood ponds and fisheries are still holding out on renovation.

As to the people of the village, in the old village area where Prem's father's farmhouse still stands, they still don't visit each other by invitation. They just walk in and out of one another's courtyards, back gardens, front doors if there are any; women simply walk straight up to neighbors' pantries and kitchens. If it is someone's daughter's wedding, it is still the wedding of a girl who belongs to the tribe and the village.

"Why did you not come back to visit here before, Mashimoni? When we were young? It's so peaceful here. It would have been such a great holiday."

Prem doesn't answer the question. She has no answer. The time for loving and growing is always right now, she thinks. Never forget the right now, this day. Never go back, never live in memory. If possible. She pats her upper left chest. A letter is tucked into her cardigan, there.

They walk on up to the pond's edge, still crumbling, ants and beetles still scurrying away in high serious haste at approaching footsteps.

"We each took one hibiscus flower from a bush somewhere here—it's probably still around, just hidden—and tied it into the borders of each other's saris. And we promised to love each other forever and always be together."

"That is nice, Mashimoni."

"We were simple village girls, you see. We didn't know all the things that city girls like you knew. But we did mean what we said and we did love each other."

Kanan's daughter listens, imagining the fifteen-year-old girl who was her mother.

"Even though my mother was a maid's daughter."

"Even though."

A little later they are back in the farmhouse—the poor teenage boy admitted defeat early and came back some time ago—in the room where Shyampiyari, Prem, and Kanan used to sleep. Saroj's room has been turned into a library, stocked with books from Sir Naren's old library that couldn't be sold with the house. Prem refused to have this room locked up, or to build a private shrine there as the Munshi suggested. "Munshi-ji," she said, a smile playing about her mouth," you knew my Mai-ji. Did she have one single religious bone in her body?"

Prem glances at Roma's face. Roma's left eye is partially closed. The area around it had to be reconstructed after the head injury she got in 12051 Henry Street the night Harish found her. Her assailant—her John for the night in Barracks parlance—was hospitalized and recovered too. At least Roma's vision was saved. Still, hers will now never be seen even as a tolerably passable face though she's still relatively young, only thirty-six.

Roma looks serious but tranquil; it relieves Prem, affirms that she may be doing the right thing. Roma will live here with her; she'll give it a try at least. Kanan's daughter may come home yet. Harish won't, and certainly she can't imagine Harish and Roma ever having married, but there are such precious memories of their years of love to remember not to forget.

And above all, when the grand future she once imagined closed its doors, the past she thought Mai-ji and Kanan stole away has let her back in. A small brick house painted a light sky blue can be seen standing—snug, not lonely—at the spot where a shanty with a thatch roof stood once, home of a poor widow and her softhearted son. When Prem looks at it she remembers a young man who wrote her ardent words of love from a battlefield. She is indeed come home, where her first loves grew and where from the windows of her father's house a little piece of her girlhood still smiles. The ancient Munshi, elated that *Bitiya Rani* is back, promises to help her run the farm and start a mango export business for as long as he lives, which seems likely to be forever. A growing country needs corn, rice, fertilizer, fresh vegetables and fruits. Droughts will come again, and famine will always lurk, but the land is still the land—pure brown gold.

"Well, set yourself up my dear," Prem tells Roma. "You have the pick of any room you like, but choose wisely!"

"Wisely?"

"Choose the spot where the morning sun comes in just the way you like it as you wake up. Where the windows open to the south wind. Where you feel not too far from people but not crowded. And where you can hear me if I fall at night and call you, old biddy that I am."

Roma wordlessly puts her arms around Prem and holds her tight for a long time. She chooses the room next to Prem's, where Shyampiyari audibly whispered tall tales to two girls forty years ago.

"Mashimoni, can we do this?"

"Do what, dear?"

"Live here?"

"Why not, dear?"

"I've never grown anything, Mashimoni. If you think about it, I actually have a long record of breaking and killing things. And you haven't either, Mashimoni."

Since that is not true—Prem grew a life, a home, a family, and three children—Prem only pats Roma on the back.

"Will things grow, Mashimoni?"

Prem looks over Roma's shoulder out the window at the horizon that cradles the land, the fields, and the new harvest. She is her father's daughter too, after all. "Oh yes my dear, things will grow, don't you worry."

CHAPTER 64

Finally, in her old bedroom Prem settles wearily into the old bed freshly made reverentially by the Munshi's daughter-in-law, a smiling, middle-aged woman who can't quite stop gawking at the daughter of this house who became the great Calcutta Lady and all. If Kanan had lived she might have looked like this woman in her middle age.

She brings the letter out from its cradle between skin and cardigan over blouse. Unfolds it. Reads.

Dear Lady Mitter (Or may I use your name, dear Prem?),

You wrote me after Roderick died that you had ever only known mothers who were demons—monsters who bled and devoured men and their own children—and that you were aghast to have to admit, finally, that I was truly one of them. Fair point. In so many ways you were Roderick's true mother. I bore him, but you raised him. We both loved him—you must believe me today when I write that we both loved him—but you loved him harder, closer, hour in and hour out, when you so easily could have abandoned him.

I sincerely grieve that I never got to know your son as you did mine. However, knowing your nature, your heart, I know that he was blessed in a mother who not only was not a monster, but who never gave him a single moment's reason to doubt his mother, to question her love, to feel abandoned. I would have loved him had I known him. Roderick used to tell me such sweet stories of growing up as brothers together

with him, of how much your son loved him, yet loved to fight with him. Sweet young boys, ours, lucky to have been together in the glory days of boyhood, when men's lives are sweetest.

But the truth, as you know dearest Prem, is that we make men, and men make wars. Then they take us as prizes or victims. We have both known such men—intimately. But at least we two—if you will allow me the honor of your circle there—can say that we made two of the best kind of men, men who didn't make wars but faced the ones thrust on them for the sakes of the women they loved. Roderick loved his "I" dearly, and in his last letter he told me how deeply he had fallen in love with his other childhood best friend—another little woman!—your very own Roma. Almost my very own. If only I'd had any luck.

I know I seemed hard and selfish—again, a monster—to you the last time we saw each other. In many ways, I had to make myself seem that way, because I was afraid. Afraid that if I didn't behave harshly, imperiously, you and Naren might not have let Roderick come to England with me. And I was afraid Roderick might decline if I seemed wishy-washy. Please forgive me, if you can, Prem. I was lonely. I was tired. I saw that I was getting old and I was afraid of lonely old age.

But Prem, let me say what emboldens me to write to one who can be entirely forgiven for resolutely closing the doors of her heart to me, even should that be the case. I write to you because we are women who know what it is to lose what we have loved best and longest. And to lose not once, but over and over again. You and I—from different worlds but shared histories—know what it is to lose the baby whose skin and limbs we protected from one little scratch or cut. Whose bodies—broken, torn, bleeding—we still had to cradle in the end in our arms or hearts. But I write to you also because you have the biggest heart of anyone I ever knew. You loved and nourished those to whom you owed nothing, not even tolerance. You loved the half-blood child of your husband and his mistress. Thank you, Prem.

My skin is white, and so is yours, but as we both know, our two white skins are worlds apart. We've had to stand looking out at each other across the vast empire that separated us, seeing only strangers, enemies. We had no choice. At least I thought so. But in truth, I now see, all the time we were sisters, lovers, mothers, and allies, and so our causes were the same. We had both hoped to see our sons become husbands and fathers, and live long and happy lives.

Dear Prem, I know you and I will not see each other again in this world. It is my fondest hope though, dearest Prem, that we'll meet again, someday, in another, better one, where we shall see the faces of everyone we loved. And that after that day, we shall never be separated again.

Yours in sincerest affection, forever,

Lilian Nandini Bhattacharya, Exit Row, 2016

Glossary

"aunties": As Rehana would call the other courtesans, her mother's "sisters"

Amritabazar Patrika: A militantly nationalist daily published in Calcutta

arrey, naa: Hindi-Bengali words meaning "oh well," and "no" meaning "yes," mixed into pidgin English

baba: Name for a small boy of privileged background

babaa and *come naa*: Pidgin exclamations and ejaculations

babu: An Indian fop or rake

bah bah: Bengali for "well, well"

baijis: Courtesans, public women, artists, and denizens of the flesh trade

Bande Mataram: The first line of a nationalistic poem by Bengali writer Bankim Chandra Chattopadhyay written in the 1870s; it subsequently became the national anthem of India during the freedom movement

banzai: Japanese soldier's battle cry: "Emperor!"

beedi: Cheap, leaf-wrapped, unfiltered tobacco

beedis: Vernacular for hand-rolled leaf cigarettes containing strong, unfiltered tobacco, usually smoked by the poor

belle de jour: French for the beauty of the day

bheto Bangali: Bhat- or rice-eating Bengali

Bilet Pherat: Bengali for "England Returned"

bitiya: Baby girl

bitiya rani: Queen daughter, or princess

blandeur: In French, insipid pretence of grandeur

bonti: Bengali word for upright steel blade embedded in wooden base that sits flat on the floor, that women use to chop things, squatting. A substititue for a knife

chhoti bahu-rani: Hindi for queenly younger sister-in-law, a term of fealty

chirobondhu: Bengali for "friends forever"

cholbey na: Can not go on

Chor Bazaar: A location in Calcutta; the name means Thieves' Market. Stolen and contraband goods were sold there

daal: Miscellaneous lentil and bean soup

danse macabre: French for Dance of the Dead

dargah: Place of prayer

dhoti: Hindi and Bengali for Indian men's traditional lower garment, a length of seamless fabric wrapped, pleated, and tucked into the waistband

Dulce est, decorum est, pro patria mori: "It is sweet and fitting to die for one's country"—Latin phrase from the Roman poet Horace that served as title of Wilfred Owen's bleak and ironic poem about World War I

Durga Puja: The festival of the great ten-armed Goddess Durga that lasts nearly ten days in autumn

eclat: French for brilliant advent

einh: A plaintive sound indicating "what" or "yes" in village vernacular

fin-de-siècle: Characteristic of the close of the nineteenth century and especially its literary and artistic climate of sophistication, world-weariness, and fashionable despair

firingi: Literally Frank, or French, later applied broadly to most westerners

Gauloises: French cigarettes

ghaghra and *angrakha*: Traditional Indian Muslim women's ceremonial skirts and bodices

gora: Indian name for "white," or "whites," or the English

gustakhi maaf, huzoor: Urdu-Hindi for "beg your pardon, master"

hai hai: Hindi or Bengali for "alas"

hakim: Doctor in Urdu

hein: A vague exclamation

infra dig: English Schoolboy shorthand for Latin infra dignitatem, "beneath dignity"

ishq, bewaafa humsafar, behuda duniya: Love, faithless lover, faithless world

jaan: Life, in Urdu

jaanu: A version of "my life" in Urdu

Jalianwalla: From Jalianwallah Bagh where in 1919 General Dyer ordered indiscriminate firing on a peaceable gathering of thousands of Indians, killing most

jamai raja: Lord son-in-law

ji huzoor:

joie de vivre: French for lust for life

kahlo bhoot: Bengali for black-skinned ghost

Kala Pani: Hindi for the black waters, namely the ocean

Kanan Debi: Literally goddess, but really more like lady, usually used to address married gentlewomen

khuku: The Bengali version of Missy Baba, and a common name for a little girl in Bengali

kothas: Residences

kumari: Miss, mademoiselle

kutcha bachcha: Half-baked baby in Hindi

La Marts: La Martiniere for Boys school, Calcutta

latak chhamak: Sashaying, inviting, explicit

Mahabharata: A fourth-century BC Sanskrit epic telling of a great war in India about a thousand years earlier. It means Great India, or the Great Epic of India

Mai-ji: What Prem calls her mother

manège: French, training of horses, carriage

mangalsutra: Necklace, worn by married Hindu women, signifying their married state

Marwari: Largely an ancient business community originating in Rajasthan in North India, but spread eventually all over India due to mercantile interests

mashimoni: In Bengali, Mashimoni is "mashi" or mother's sister graced with "moni," or gemstone; precious mother's sister

mem: Hindi or Bengali abbreviation of "memsahib," itself short for "Madam Sahib"

memsahib: Short for Madam Sahib

missy baba: A young girl from a well-to-do, westernized family

mujrah: Private singing and sometimes dancing entertainments by celebrated public women, an Indian version of the Salon

nahi huzoor: Urdu-Hindi for "no, master"

nautankis, shikar, and *kusti*: Raunchy female dancers, hunting, and mud wrestling

nawabs: Indian title for princes and potentates who had served under the Mughal emperor, usually in provinces, and whom the British later mostly stripped of all but titular authority and nominal possessions

oyay: A rude call like "you!"

paan: Betel leaf, areca nuts, and slaked lime paste

padhhe-likhhe: "Reading-writing"; literate

parganahs: Districts or zones

pati bhakti: Sanskrit for wifely devotion

payals: Tinkling anklets

poorna swaraj: Full independence

prasad: The food offered to the goddess and then distributed among the worshippers

Presidency College: Elite Calcutta college for Indians founded in the nineteenth century by the British

pukka brown sahib: A deracinated, westernized Indian man. Pukka means solid or fully formed, as in architecture and fruit; a pukka sahib was a colonized person who almost perfectly imitated the English, like Henry Babington Macaulay's predicted race that would be Indian in skin and blood but English in manners and morals

rotis: Hindi for thin Indian flatbread

saal leaf: General vernacular for tree leaves of a beige-brown color when aged

salwar kameeze: Indian women's traditional tunics and pants

sang froid: French for self-possession or imperturbability especially under strain

Satyagraha: Mahatma Gandhi's primary slogan for the anti-colonial movement: Truth Above All

sepoy: How the British pronounced "sipahi," meaning soldier in Hindi/Urdu

shirimati: Akin to lady, or madam

sori chhori: Knife wife

Statesman: Prominent Calcutta English-language newspaper started by the English but still running

Glossary

tabla: Traditional small percussive drum

tawaifi: Complex, semiclassical style of music nurtured and perfected by courtesans from the fifteenth-sixteenth century onward that ended up influencing a lot of Indian film music

terai: Lower Himalayan hillside where tea is grown

thumris: Probably the closest comparison would be as the Urdu version of the medieval French *chansons d'amour*

Umricah: America

zenana: Women's private quarters, though for the working classes such privacy was less common

Acknowledgements

My greatest inspiration for writing this novel is my son Khoka Myers; he knows why. We were misty-eyed and tongue-tied after I read the last chapter of *Love's Garden* in draft out loud to him, and then he nodded Yes. My kindest supporter and prime instigator for doing the work, and making the best of hardest choices, is Leo Hartman, friend and partner. My invaluable ally and life and writing coach Patricia Murphy, a talented novelist herself, showed me that the writing life is possible even as I insisted it was only for others. I have no words of thanks good enough for my debt to these writing teachers and mentors: Chitra Banerjee Divakaruni, Tiphany Yanique, Meg Wolitzer, Joan Silber, Hernan Diaz, Maud Casey, Kathleen Spivack, Mita Mitra, Kristina Marie Darling, Rita Banerjee, and Diana Szokolyai. Nivea Castro, Tori Reynolds, Angela Ajayi, Laurie Thomas, Indira Ganesan, Mia Alvar, Danton Remoto, Shona Jackson, Catalina Bartlett, Marco Portales, Trisha Malik, Alicia Link, Joanna Tam, Mousumi Rao nee Sen, Tazim Jamal, Sarbani Bose, Vivek and Dolly Ahuja, Diana Davila, David Morgan, Susan Lee, Giselle Mora, Renu Juneja, Scott Coon, David Samuel Levinson, Jo Chandy, and my sister Shalini Bhattacharya—you all know I would be nowhere and nothing without you.

My sincerest thanks go to Voices of Our Nation Arts, Sarah Lawrence College, the Cambridge Writers Workshop, the Southampton Summer Writers Workshop, the Vermont Studio Center, the Bread Loaf Writers Workshop, and the English department at Texas A&M University for support and sustenance when I most needed them. My publishers at Aubade—Joe, Vonda, and Cosette Puckett—have been the most fantastic readers, editors, and cheerleaders. I thank you from the bottom of my heart for taking me on. Warmest thanks also to Kristina Marie Darling for being the world's most crackerjack publicist imaginable.

Last but not least, you, my foremothers, who stand behind me in the long, dim hallway of lost time, with love lighting up your eyes and the dimness of forgotten histories, this book is about you and wouldn't have lived without you.

CPSIA information can be obtained
at www.ICGtesting.com
Printed in the USA
BVHW040541191020
591291BV00014B/439